MESSENGERS OF HEALING

From the Hunters' experiences:
An easy way to win the lost.
How to heal the sick.

CHARLES & FRANCES HUNTER

RICHARD & BRENDA YOUNG

WHITAKER
HOUSE

MESSENGERS OF HEALING

ISBN: 978-1-60374-106-4
Printed in the United States of America

Whitaker House
1030 Hunt Valley Circle
New Kensington, PA 15068
www.whitakerhouse.com

Library of Congress Cataloging-in-Publication Data

Young, Richard, 1952–
Messengers of healing / by Richard and Brenda Young.
p. cm.
Summary: "A detailed biography of Charles and Frances Hunter's journeys from spiritual apathy to leading one of the nation's most well-known healing ministries"—Provided by publisher.
ISBN 978-1-60374-106-4 (trade pbk. : alk. paper) 1. Hunter, Charles, 1920– 2. Hunter, Frances Gardner, 1916– 3. Healers—United States—Biography. 4. Evangelists—United States—Biography. I. Young, Brenda, 1952– II. Title.

BT732.56.H86Y68 2009
269'.20922—dc22
[B]

2008051580

1 2 3 4 5 6 7 8 9 10 11 12 W 16 15 14 13 12 11 10 09

ACKNOWLEDGMENTS

This must be acknowledged as a labor of love. Our lives have been changed by the ministry of Charles and Frances Hunter. These two people are a walking illustration of the greatness of our Lord Jesus Christ. Since we first called their office over fifteen years ago, they have been guides and mentors to us in ministry and faithfulness. Charles and Frances have been there for us. I know that God has no grandchildren. We are all children of God. But Charles and Frances have been encouragers and prayer warriors for us in every situation, personal and professional alike. We will thank God for them for the rest of our lives.

We would like to thank Virginia Kite for her contribution to this book. Virginia stepped in and edited the book to speed the release date. She has worked with Frances for many years and made unique contributions that only someone with that knowledge and experience could have made. Without her dedicated help and assistance, it could have easily been another year before the book would have seen bookstores. Everyone wanted to see this book released as soon as possible, but things were complicated. Virginia stepped in and rescued everyone. We owe a debt of gratitude to Virginia that we can never repay.

The marvelous help from everyone at Whitaker House must also be acknowledged. This was our first time to work with editor Jonathan Tennent, and we thank him very much for everything he did. Christine Whitaker is one of God's angels. We also want to thank Bob Whitaker for his faith in us. Everyone should have the opportunity to work with such a great Christian man.

Finally, for me, this pays a debt much past due. Brenda has been a vital part of every book I have ever written. My process is to write chapters. My background is in academics. I do great research. I get the facts right. But the details need polishing. Brenda is the polisher. She takes my words and makes them sound exciting. She sends the work back to me for rewrite and then to Whitaker. Without her polishing, I don't know if anything would ever be published or sold. She is my partner in life and in every other way. I thank God for thirty-six years and pray for thirty-six more.

—Richard Young

Contents

Foreword *11*

Introduction *13*

1. Frances—Before Charles *15*

2. Love and Marriage *27*

3. Frances Encounters a Living God *41*

4. Charles—Before Frances *55*

5. Souls, Books, and Suitcases *69*

6. A Divine Love Affair *81*

7. The Happy Hunters *95*

8. Partnering with the Holy Spirit *107*

9. Miracle Ministry *127*

10. Worldwide Healing Explosions *137*

11. Holy Laughter *149*

12. Take a Census of the World *163*

13. The Astrodome Retires in Glory *181*

14. Until Jesus Comes *189*

Conclusion *201*

About the Authors *203*

Foreword

What an inspirational story of two legendary figures in the body of Christ!

Within theses pages is the story of the extraordinary walk of faith of Charles and Frances Hunter, two people whom I treasure both as friends and as influential Christian leaders.

Most people know Charles and Frances Hunter as "The Happy Hunters," two of the most anointed healing evangelists in the world. This book offers an honest behind-the-scenes account of the life experiences of this amazing couple. You'll discover how their faith in God helped them overcome many of the difficulties and challenges that all of us experience.

As I read their biography, I was inspired again by the Hunters' commitment and dedication to one another and to sharing with the world the healing power of Jesus Christ.

They are truly modern-day "heroes of faith" whose story will inspire and motivate you to seek a more intimate walk with Jesus Christ.

—Marilyn Hickey

INTRODUCTION

Two young people had become acquainted with each other in a rural area in southern Illinois. More than casually attracted, the hopeful young Fred Fuller was so intent on capturing the approval of Dessie Bradilla Pyles that, making sure she was watching, he took a sprint across an open field and made a flying leap over a four-foot-tall livestock fence. Much to his shock, he lost his footing, landed with an uncomfortable splat, and slid right through a pile of freshly dropped cow manure. Initially worried about how badly her prospective beau might be hurt, Dessie took just a moment to confirm that only his pride had been injured and then tried desperately to muffle her laughter!

The two were soon wed and became the parents of a beautiful baby daughter, Kathleen. They had little to offer but love as they struggled to make ends meet, living off the meager salaries they made as schoolteachers.

Before Kathleen was a year old, the Fullers were expecting their second child. It was 1916—a year of tragedy, progress, and promise. The first global war, a polio epidemic, and a strained economy were in the news daily. On the bright side, mechanical refrigerators, windshield wipers, and other useful inventions brought hope to otherwise gloomy days.

On May 8 of this extraordinary year, Frances Eileen Fuller was born. As a child, Frances was challenged rather than dismayed by her family's battles with sickness and poverty, and she proved early on that she could accomplish anything she set her mind to. She treated criticism as a stimulus. She thrived when faced with obstacles. A goal setter and workaholic, she had an attitude that carried her through disappointments and over obstacles until, one day, she realized that all her talents and accomplishments did not fill the great hole in her inner being.

Half a nation away, a little boy was growing up in the breathtaking Chama River valley of New Mexico. Charles Hunter was born to able-bodied and strong-willed descendents of the hardy pioneers who had built the West. Among his earliest recollections are his father's colorful language and how, after getting saved, his language was transformed and he began a relentless search for God's plan for his life. Charles learned from his hardworking family the value of making wise use of both time and money. His responsibilities as a farm boy, coupled with a drive to make a better life, developed characteristics that would qualify him for the work for which God was preparing him.

Frances describes herself as a wild sinner who fell in love with Jesus, while Charles testifies that he spent nearly thirty-one years in a spiritual desert of religious activity.

The faith journey of Charles and Frances Hunter is tracked through the pages of this book. You will find it an absolute joy to read about how God orchestrated every event in their lives so that one day, when a tall, handsome widower appeared in the meeting of a wild, lady preacher, God's vision for a world-changing ministry through them would be realized.

Chapter One

Frances

Before Charles

The long, dismal winter of 1916 at last forfeited to spring, and May flowers swayed outside Fred and Dessie Fuller's tiny, one-room, dirt-floor log cabin. Oblivious to the struggles of a world at war, the young expectant mother was consumed with her own struggle—the birth of her second child.

Parents of nineteen-month-old Kathleen, the hopeful father and mother looked forward to the love and laughter of another baby. But they knew something was wrong. Labor had begun more than two months early. Fred paced the floor anxiously as the local midwife tended to his wife. There was no doctor in Saratoga, Illinois, a town of twelve.

As the midwife quickened the pace of her instructions, the nervous father heard a lengthy series of moans, escalating in volume until, suddenly, there was silence. The quiet seemed unbearable to Fred until the midwife finally motioned for him to come to her side. He saw in her hands a slightly wrinkled, grayish object that looked more like a miniature grown-up than a baby.

In a hushed voice, the midwife told him, "It's a little girl. I'm sorry, she's not going to make it; I'm going to try to save your wife."

Fred stood in a daze as he watched the midwife wrap the tiny infant in the warm blanket that her mother had lovingly made while waiting for the child's arrival. Concerned about the immediate care that the mother needed, the midwife took a quick look around and noticed a shoe box on the dresser. It was the perfect size for the tiny, two-pound bundle, and she positioned the baby in the box, tucking soft folds of blanket around the motionless form so that it could die in peace. She quickly turned back to attend to the baby's mother.

Fred stroked his wife's hand as she sobbed softly, realizing that she was never going to see her new daughter play with her big sister. But something was happening inside that lonely shoe box. An incredibly determined baby girl, Frances Eileen, was struggling with all her might to make her first sound. Something inside her was screaming, "I will live and not die!"

Busily tending to the baby's mother, the midwife didn't notice the miracle taking place in the shoe box—until something that sounded like the slightest squeal reached her ears from the direction of the dresser.

On May 8, 1916, this little rural family grew from three to four, and the sunbeam that filtered through a log-framed window illuminated a cardboard shoe box filled with life.

Times of Change

As the national economy struggled, many rural families moved to the cities in order to survive. Small towns shrank to even smaller sizes, and schools closed. Fred and Dessie, both teachers, found themselves without children to teach, so they moved from Saratoga to Rockford, and then to Chicago, where Fred got a job with Bauer and Black, a nationwide surgical supply house.

Fred rented a small, single room in a boardinghouse for himself and his family. The room had only a sink, a stove, and a single spring bed. Fred and his wife slept on the lumpy bed. The girls slept on a pallet of thick blankets and quilts on the cool, wooden floor.

The girls slept on a pallet of thick blankets and quilts on the cool, wooden floor.

Every night, Fred tucked Frances and Kay into their makeshift bed, making sure the edges of upper and lower bedding were rolled together so the cold air from the floor would not chill them. After their daddy had woven an exciting bedtime tale for them and had given them a final tucking in and good-night kiss, they would snuggle happily together under homemade quilts. It never occurred to the little girls to complain. They were grateful to be together.

It was a cloudy Chicago morning. Shivering in the crisp autumn wind, Frances tugged at Fred's coat sleeve while Kay gazed worriedly at her father's face. A big machine had come to their apartment. Two men had picked up their mother and put her in the ambulance. With voice quivering, Frances asked, "Where is mommy going?"

Kay patted her sister's hand and said, "It'll be okay, Toodie." As a toddler, Kay had pronounced "Sugar Pie" as "Toodie Pie," a nickname that stuck with Frances until she married Charles.

Moving from place to place is exhausting—mentally, physically, and emotionally. Frances' mother had never recovered her full strength after moving to Chicago, and she succumbed to a dreaded plague of the era—tuberculosis. Frances was just four years old when the ambulance came.

For the next four years, Frances' mother lived in a tuberculosis sanatorium, leaving her husband to care for the two little girls. At this time, most people didn't hire babysitters; they left children with family members or grandparents. Fred had no one with whom he could entrust his girls. So, each morning before leaving for work, he gave the two little girls very strict instructions: "Stay in your room! Do not go outside until I return!"

When summer came, Fred sent Frances to stay on a farm with her paternal grandparents. She thought it was great fun and very nice of her parents to send them to the farm every summer. In reality, Fred had no one to care for the girls in the city and had trouble feeding them, as well. The farm was an answer to both problems. Fred Fuller was all but a single father, and he had great problems taking care of a sick wife and two little girls while working to provide for their needs. But he did the best he could to care for his two girls and his ailing wife.

Frances' big sister Kathleen tried to help, but she was only a little girl herself. Out of necessity, the girls learned to cook early in life. One day, they decided to cook oatmeal, so they boiled a pot of water and put a whole package of oatmeal into it. It grew and grew, so they got a larger pot. It still continued to grow, until finally, they had filled every pot in the kitchen with oatmeal!

Frances and Kathleen saw their mother only on Sundays, when their father would take them to the sanatorium. They were not allowed to go inside but had to remain outside the locked gates of the fenced-in area around the building until, after what seemed endless waiting, their mother would come to the window and wave to them. The two sisters, thrust into womanhood with no mother at home, grew in maturity and responsibility beyond their years.

Without maternal interaction, Frances' memories of her mother grew vague. She could never remember her mother kissing her. Later, with the maturity of adulthood, she realized that it was because her mother did not want to risk giving tuberculosis to her children. However, her relationship with her father was very positive.

Meaningful Memories

Fred was a gifted storyteller. Frances and Kay anxiously anticipated their father's stories at night before they went to sleep. His imaginative tales took them out of their bleak surroundings and into a colorful world of amazing places and thrilling characters. In later years, Frances applied that special gift to her life's calling of making Jesus alive and exciting to listeners all over the world.

In later years, Frances applied the gift of storytelling to her life's calling of making Jesus alive and exciting to listeners all over the world.

Starting school is always a monumental event in a young child's life. When Kay was six years old, she could hardly wait to begin first grade. But what was to be done with her four-year-old sister? Fred kept thinking until he came up with a solution, but he wasn't sure if it would be accepted by the principal. He went down to the school and explained that he had no one to care for his young daughter. Drawing a deep breath, he then asked the principal and teacher if Frances could come to school with her older sister. The office clock ticked loudly as he sat waiting for an answer.

With a smile, the teacher glanced in the direction of the principal, who nodded, and an agreement was reached. Frances could come to

Kathleen's classroom with her if, and only if, she sat still and did not open her mouth.

Elated, Fred relayed the information to his daughters. Every day thereafter, four-year-old Frances was tugged alongside her sister through paths often piled high with snow to a welcoming schoolhouse. Many years later, multitudes of people worldwide who heard the exuberant praise, teaching, and prayers of Frances Hunter would have a difficult time believing that she spent her first year of school sitting in a classroom without making a sound.

Daddy's Girls

Fred had a special compassion for his girls. He knew the burden of having no mother to comfort and guide them was a heavy one for children so young. Frances recalls that an aunt once told her bluntly that her sister Kay was her father's favorite. Frances immediately responded that the aunt was wrong and that she was her daddy's favorite!

Fred made both of his daughters feel like they were the greatest gifts on earth to him, and he took every opportunity to demonstrate his love for them. His impartiality and tenderness would one day help Frances relate to her loving Father God and would help her communicate that incredible love to every person she met.

When Frances was eight years old, her father was transferred to St. Louis, where he rented a small apartment for his family. Her mother decided not to go back into a sanatorium but to live at home. However, she was still very weak. This was when Frances learned to cook and Kay learned to clean the dishes.

Introduction to Church but Not to Jesus

One weekend, Fred and his wife discussed the need for the girls to become associated with a church. In those days, people who were unchurched were considered lower-class and were looked upon with disdain. Fred and Dessie dutifully dressed their daughters in their best clothes, and the family joined the nearby Methodist church.

On the first morning at church, in the dim auditorium with its majestic stained glass window, Frances took in the ethereal atmosphere of choir anthems and long pastoral prayers. She felt something that she describes as "the heartbeat of God." At the age of eight, she did not understand what she was feeling, but it left an indelible impression on her and marked a milestone in her life.

In all the time that the girls obeyed their parents and regularly attended church services, no one ever said a word about a personal relationship with Jesus.

The pastor was so excited to have the Fuller family join the church that he turned to the congregation and exclaimed, "Isn't this a wonderful family? A mother and daddy and their two little girls have joined our church today!" However, what Frances remembers to this day is that the pastor failed to mention the importance of inviting Jesus into your heart. In all the time that the girls obeyed their parents and regularly attended church services, no one ever said a word about a personal relationship with Jesus.

Growing Pains

With an irritated grimace and stomp of her foot, Toodie stared into the mirror. "I wish I could cut off my legs!" she exclaimed.

Even in grade school, Frances stood out among her classmates—in fact, she towered over them, much to her frustration. Worse yet, she even outgrew most of the boys in her class. How she wished she could be petite, graceful, and cute like other girls. Instead, she saw herself as a big, clumsy cow who was like a bull in a china shop. Some of her relatives did little to help her self-image.

Frances' Aunt Cora was not known for diplomacy. "Now, where is my darling little Kathleen?" she inquired as soon as she walked through the door one day. Spotting Kay, she marveled at what a beautiful young girl she was becoming, what lovely skin she had, and what gorgeous hair framed her perfect little face.

Frances stood politely by, waiting for her aunt to notice her and tell her how pretty she was. She was a relative, after all, and everybody is beautiful to her own family members. After what seemed like an eternity, Aunt Cora turned to her and, in a strange voice, asked, "This is Frances?"

Frances felt a lump rising in her throat, but she pushed it back and tilted her face up toward her aunt's. Straightening her shoulders, she proudly proclaimed, "I may not be P-R-E-T-T-Y, but I sure am S-M-A-R-T." Frances did not take a backseat to anyone. Her aunt's words remained with her throughout her lifetime as an incident where she could have felt sorry for herself but instead chose to believe in herself.

Pass the Potatoes, Please

Working as a traveling salesman for Bauer and Black enabled Fred to meet his family's basic needs and to save a little money each week. The stock market was thriving, so Fred decided to take his nest egg and invest toward a better life for his girls. Instead of leading them to wealth, however, the stock market crashed on October 29, 1929, causing Fred, like so many others, to lose all his savings.

Not one to wallow in discouragement, Fred kept working his sales routes. There were few sales, though, because the economy was suffering. At thirteen, Frances remembers that they were not just poor; they were poor, poor, poor! One month, their income was so meager that the only thing Fred could afford that would allow them to eat for the whole month was a big burlap sack of potatoes. They ate boiled potatoes with oleo for breakfast, boiled potatoes with oleo for lunch, and boiled potatoes with oleo for dinner. It was not a buffet, but potatoes have a way of filling hungry stomachs!

They did enjoy one luxury, however. Every Sunday, Fred would fill the car with gas, which cost twenty-one cents per gallon, and take the girls on a short drive in the country. Before they returned home, each of them would get a "chicken dinner." The girls would tell their school mates the next day that their daddy had taken them out for a chicken dinner on Sunday. What they didn't say was that there was a penny candy bar by the name of "Chicken Dinner," and that was the treat that their daddy had given them. They did not even know what a restaurant was!

A Father's Gift

Frances found that being tall for her age did have some advantages, such as looking older than she really was. At twelve, she could reach the gas and brake pedals on her father's car. Much to her astonishment, once, while driving on a rural country road, her father pulled over, handed her the keys, and said, "Come on, let's see if you can drive this car!"

Without hesitation, Frances traded seats and, for about a mile, drove the 1924 Buick at the blazing speed of nearly ten miles per hour. She gripped the steering wheel with all her might as the car sashayed from side to side, but at the end of her ride, she had not killed anyone or driven off the road into a ditch. More noteworthy, Frances' faith in herself soared. She knew that if she could drive a car as a twelve-year-old, she could do anything she set her mind to.

Frances knew that if she could drive a car as a twelve-year-old, she could do anything she set her mind to.

Fred's encouragement and belief in his daughter, not just on this monumental day but throughout Frances' childhood, cultivated within her an attitude of strength and confidence that would empower her all of her life.

If You Can Do It, I Can Do It!

A young Spanish man came to Frances' high school to put on a typing demonstration. It was the very first time Frances—and almost everyone else—had ever seen a typewriter. Frances watched in amazement as the young man placed a single sheet of white paper into the machine, rapidly pressed the keys, and turned out complete sentences in a matter of seconds. He proudly proclaimed that he was able to type at the rate of one hundred and twenty-five words per minute! That was almost too much for the mind to comprehend, but Frances decided that if this young man could type at that rate, she could do it, too.

The school formed a typing class, and Frances immediately enrolled in it. She was quick to realize that typing was much more difficult than she had imagined. The Spanish man had made it look so easy!

Undaunted and highly motivated, Frances asked the typing instructor if she could stay after school each day to practice. The teacher readily agreed, but after a few days of Frances diligently appearing to practice, and with no indication that she was going to stop, the teacher reneged. She had other responsibilities that took priority over remaining after school to supervise an enthusiastic young typist.

When Frances was no longer able to type after school, a brilliant idea came to her, and she located all the department stores in downtown St. Louis that sold typewriters. Day after day, she would save the dime that her father gave her for lunch and spend it to take the bus downtown and practice her typing. When she arrived downtown, she would walk into one of the stores and find a salesman. She would say to him, "I am interested in typewriters." Frances was careful not to lie to them, and she didn't say she was interested in buying a typewriter. She would just ask, "May I have a piece of paper?" The salesman, happy to allow her to test his product, would hand her a sheet of paper.

She would then stand in front of the typewriter and type, "Now is the time for all good men to come to the aid of their country." Over and over, she would type the phrase until the front side of the paper was filled. Then she would turn the paper over and type all the way down the back side of the page, "Now is the time for all good men to come to the aid of their country." With both sides filled, she would thank the salesman with a beaming smile, leave, and proceed down the street to the next department store to practice.

Frances Eileen had learned how to set a goal, believe in herself, and make a way for that goal to be realized. Through her persistence and initiative, she eventually was able to type one hundred twenty-five words per minute.

It has often been observed that children who live with adversity grow into adults of strong character. Frances was proving herself with every year that she lived. She did not know her future, but a loving God was faithful to oversee every step she took. She was tenacious, and He assisted her with every goal she set for herself. At sixteen, she pursued what she considered a challenge by a typewriter salesman,

---

Frances was tenacious, and God assisted her with every goal she set for herself.

---

telling herself, "If he can do it, I can do it." Later in her life, Frances would use her typing skills to start a business that initially would support her children but ultimately would result in writing and publishing life-changing books that would be translated into many of the world's languages.

Safety in Numbers

Frances' father laid ground rules for his girls to follow when they had grown old enough to think about going out with young men. Very simply, he stated they could go only on "double dates." Kathleen, being prettier, was told that Frances would accompany her on all of her excursions, and that the boy Kathleen was seeing would have to bring along a friend of Frances' age to entertain her.

A wonderful thing happened as a result of Fred's rules: Frances got to know all the boys in her class as Kathleen's boyfriends would choose them to tag along. When they spent time together, the boys realized that Frances had a sparkling personality, and they always enjoyed being with her. Frances' list of friends grew. The girl who had towered over them in their childhood now had a magnetism that drew boys and girls alike to her. She became a leader among her peers, was elected to Student Council, and graduated as a member of the National Honor Society.

Ambitious and Determined

Just prior to Frances' seventeenth birthday, her mother died. Fred, Kathleen, and Frances were with her as she looked from one girl to the other and told them, "You girls, be good girls." Dessie would have been proud had she been able to be truly involved in her daughters' lives as they grew. She would have seen their strength of character, the lifelong devotion they had for each other, and the attitude of doing all within their power to achieve their goals.

When Frances graduated from high school in 1933, even with her Honor Society achievement, there was no hope of going to college. But the Great Depression was not going to deter her from doing something with her life, and it would have to be something that she loved, not just a mundane job in a cannery or coat factory with no challenge or future.

She enrolled in a nearby secretarial school so she could improve the skills that she knew would open doors for a desirable job. As soon as she graduated, she went to work for a small payday loan company, where she remained for three years until it was sold to another company and many positions were terminated, including hers.

In 1936, the worldwide depression was in full force. Frances was unemployed and on her own, and no one was hiring new workers. Thousands who had lost their jobs stood in food lines for hours just to bring home a few staple items for their families.

St. Louis was the regional headquarters for Southwestern Bell Telephone Company. Frances had heard that Southwestern Bell was a good place to work, but she had been told that there was no chance of getting a job there. The facility even had a large sign up that said "NOT HIRING" in bold letters. Being told that she had no chance of getting hired just made Frances' mind start working. She thrived on challenges, and she was not about to take "no" for an answer.

On a dank fall morning, rain drizzled on long queues of unemployed workers, waiting at factories and establishments throughout the city for their turn at receiving some sign of hope for a job. Outside the towering Southwestern Bell administration building, a young man dressed in a freshly pressed Western Union uniform rang the buzzer for a delivery. The supervisor who greeted him returned to her office to open an impressive telegram that stated, "If you would be interested in talking to the fastest typist that will ever work for your organization, contact me." Frances' name and telephone number followed.

The giant company was intrigued by the telegram. They wanted to see who would have the nerve to write a message like that when there was an obvious "NOT HIRING" sign outside. Frances received a call for an interview, strode confidently in for her appointment, and was hired on the spot for the secretarial pool. She was twenty years old. She would soon be promoted to secretary for the chief accountant of the entire St. Louis division.

Chapter Two

Love and Marriage

Fred shook his head in amusement, smiled at his daughter, and said, "All right, you go ahead, and just be careful to come home in one piece." Frances had just convinced him to let her and three friends use his new car for the first vacation she had ever had. How could Fred say no to his little girl?

Four excited young women packed up the car and headed west to the Grand Canyon. They were looking forward to having the time of their lives. However, after riding a mule down steep, narrow trails along the side of the great canyon and then back up, Frances was not sure she would ever be able to walk normally again!

The girls left Arizona and continued to be inspired and exhilarated by breathtaking scenery as they drove to a Colorado dude ranch, where another great adventure awaited them. One of the other tourists visiting the ranch was a young accountant from Chicago named Larry Steder.

When the girls arrived, they found four good-looking guys sitting on the porch of the ranch house. Frances gave them her biggest smile and asked, "Would you like to carry our luggage up to our rooms?" The response was a resounding "No."

Love in the Air

The four girls carried their luggage upstairs themselves, but when dinnertime came, those four boys were waiting outside their door to go down to dinner with them. The one who introduced himself as Larry

Frances (third from the bottom) riding a mule to the bottom of the Grand Canyon in 1942.

Steder caught Frances' eye and soon captured her heart. She was thrilled to learn that he was from Chicago and not distant Oregon or Montana! Over the next few months, Larry and Frances took turns driving to see each other. One weekend, she and a girlfriend would go to Chicago; the next, Larry and a friend would come to St. Louis.

Frances and Larry realized they were in love, but before they could think about marriage, two events shook their world. First, Frances' beloved father died from the dreaded tuberculosis that had robbed her of her mother. Second, on December 7, 1941, Japan bombed Pearl Harbor. Larry immediately enlisted in the U.S. Navy and was sent to the Navy Pier in New York. Frances moved to Chicago to be close to Larry's parents and developed a beautiful relationship with Larry's tiny but dynamic mother. Mrs. Steder was an accomplished cook and taught Frances many of her cooking secrets. Larry and Frances were finally married in Chicago on September 19, 1942.

When Frances moved to Chicago, she decided that, since her father had worked for Bauer and Black, she would like a job there, too. In the spot where her application said, "Type of work you want," she wrote, "I will work for one week with no pay, and at the end of the week, you can decide where I belong."

The company called Frances and placed her in the stenographic pool, where they had a machine attached to the typewriter to show how many keys had been pressed during a given week. At the end of the week, Frances had typed more than anybody ever had in the history of Bauer and Black. Frances was not only fast, but she was also a perfectionist in all aspects of the letters that she produced. She believed in always giving 100 percent. At the end of the week, the company made her secretary to the general sales manager.

Shortly afterward, she worked for Thomas Harwood, the CEO of Bauer and Black at that time. She was so impressed with him and his work habits that she later named her son, Thomas, after him.

Wartime Changes

After getting married, Frances moved to New York to be near her husband. They did not know how long he would be stationed there, but they wanted to spend every possible moment together. She easily transferred to Bauer and Black's New York office, where she quickly advanced to become secretary to the president of the company.

Late in 1944, Larry received orders to transfer to a base in San Francisco, three thousand miles away. The Navy didn't waste any time with transfers, and Larry called Frances with instructions to grab everything she could fit into their two suitcases, go to the train station, watch for him, and get on the same train that he got on.

Frances had just enough money to buy a train ticket to Chicago. She followed Larry's instructions to call his mother and have her meet them in Chicago with enough money to complete the train trip to California. Larry's mother gave Frances extra money for a sleeping berth, which the couple was able to use for the long trip.

Larry had obtained permission from a superior officer to sleep in the berth with his wife, because the night before, a Navy wife had been murdered while riding on the train. In the middle of the night, the exhausted couple was awakened by the glaring flashlight of a Navy MP who barked at them, "What are you doing in here?"

Larry responded sleepily, "I'm just traveling with my wife." The MP asked for proof that they were legally married. Frances, who had learned to carry her marriage license with her wherever she went, was able to produce the evidence the MP had demanded. The rest of their travel to San Francisco was, thankfully, uneventful.

Frances and Larry wanted a child desperately but were unable to conceive. Once settled in San Francisco, Frances underwent three minor surgeries and became pregnant. She asked God for a brown-eyed boy who would look just like his daddy. Five months into the pregnancy, Larry received the orders they dreaded—it was time to ship out. During World War II, servicemen were allowed to move their families back home to be close to relatives, if they desired, so Larry took Frances to his mother's home in Chicago and then left with his unit for Okinawa.

This Baby Has No Head!

On September 20, 1945, at three o'clock in the morning, Frances sat straight up in bed as an excruciating pain ran across her back. Then, there was another, and another. Frances had no idea what labor pains were like, so she woke up her mother-in-law, who called the doctor. The doctor confirmed that she was in labor and told them, for the family's convenience, that since Frances' father-in-law was to be operated on the next morning in a certain hospital, it would be better for them to go there than to the hospital Frances was planning on using for the birth of her baby. When you're in labor, you don't argue, you just want to get to the hospital! So they sped to the designated facility.

Once settled in her room, Frances was instructed by the nurse to walk up and down the hall to prevent a lengthy labor. As Frances was attempting to get out of bed, a young Chinese intern entered the room to examine her. Lying flat on her back with birth pangs intensifying, Frances was relieved to put off walking for a few minutes. She tried to relax as he began his examination, and then nearly went into shock when the intern screamed, "This baby has no head!"

> *The intern shouted frantically again, this time louder than before, "This baby has no head!"*

Frances' mind tried to comprehend what the intern had said. She didn't know anything about giving birth, but she did know that babies are supposed to have heads! *What will my baby look like with no head? What will people say? Will they stare? How will the baby walk with no head?* Interrupting her whirling thoughts, the intern shouted frantically again, this time louder than before, "This baby has no head!"

By this time, a nurse who had heard him screaming from down the hall came running into the room. She thought she might have misheard him and asked him to repeat what he had been saying. His voice cracked from strain as he screeched the words again: "The baby has no head!" The nurse helped women give birth every day. She gave the intern a "get quiet right now" glare and examined Frances herself.

The room was silent as Frances and the intern awaited her verdict. Frances held her breath until the nurse straightened and announced, "This baby definitely has a head, but it is coming breech," which meant that the baby was coming out bottom first.

Four hours later, Frances gave birth to the beautiful baby boy she had prayed for, and whose blue eyes would soon change to brown like his daddy's. With the birth of Tom Steder, Frances felt that her cup was running over.

Frances and her first child, Tom, in 1945.

Life and Death

Larry returned from Okinawa in the fall of 1945, and he was discharged by the Navy shortly after Tom's birth. Frances could hardly wait to meet him and place his baby son in his arms. The accounting firm where he had worked before the war had saved his job for him, and it was not long before they bought a small home on the south side of Chicago, from which Larry commuted daily to the office. The little family of three looked as though they had nothing but bright days ahead of them.

Then, something unusual began to happen. Larry began to hemorrhage from the nose. He underwent surgery at the Veterans Hospital and returned home, feeling well. But before long, the hemorrhaging started again. He returned to the hospital, where they diagnosed him with cancer of the brain. He went through many serious operations and, after each one, was able to go back to work. Finally, the day came when the hemorrhaging could not be helped, and Larry was admitted into the hospital. The doctor told Frances that he had only two months to live.

The accounting company had continued to pay Larry during the times he was unable to work. But after the doctors gave Frances the news that her husband had no longer than two months to live, she returned the paycheck with a note saying, "You are mailing us this paycheck because you think Larry is coming back to work. I regret to tell you that the doctors have told me he is going to die from brain cancer. Therefore, I cannot accept this check, so I am returning it to you." Her integrity would not allow her to keep the money.

The company immediately called Frances and asked how long Larry was expected to live. They told her that they were sending the check back to her and would continue paying him so that she would be able to collect his life insurance. Frances' heart swelled with gratitude that a business would reach out to them so compassionately. She later realized how God had moved on her behalf and how lovingly He had always watched over her, even when she had not been saved.

During Larry's decline in health, Frances, prompted by her parents' precedent, felt that it was important for them to join a church. Deep within her, she knew that this was more than a social necessity—it was her way of reaching out to God. She also was concerned for Larry's spiritual well-being. He had never attended a church service in his life. Although no one had ever spoken to either of them about the saving grace of Jesus Christ, she felt that joining a church would provide Larry with spiritual strength. The bottom line was that she didn't want him to

Deep within her, Frances knew that joining a church was more than a social necessity—it was her way of reaching out to God.

die without belonging to a church—a forerunner of her passion to make sure that every individual she would ever come into contact with would belong to Jesus.

With a sick husband and an infant son, Frances realized that she could not work a traditional nine-to-five job away from the home. She underwent the necessary training to become a cosmetic consultant for Peggy Newton Cosmetics, a precursor to companies such as Mary Kay and Avon. Frances could do much of her preparation at home and be away for only short periods of time to hold parties in ladies' homes. Her outgoing personality, caring attitude for everyone, and natural determination to succeed propelled her to become the top cosmetic consultant in the entire state of Illinois.

Larry was in the Veterans Hospital when the doctors told him that he was going to die. He had asked them to release him because he wanted to die at home. Frances brought him home, where she tended to him as much as possible in the daytime and hired a male nurse to care for him at night.

As she gently stroked Larry's hand and gazed at his pale face, Frances knew in her spirit and could see with her eyes that Larry was nearing death, but that did not mean she was going to accept it. She was determined to spend every possible moment with her husband. She spent many nights sleeping in little Tom's bedroom, next to Larry's room, so that the two of them could be near him. She wanted to do everything she could to keep him alive. She did not want to think about what she would do without him.

One night, Larry's breathing became extremely labored. It seemed that every breath took all the energy he possessed. Frances was standing next to his bed and trying to will him to live when his breathing stopped. Frances couldn't believe it. She was not going to let him die! She shouted at the top of her lungs, "Don't go! Don't go!"

Suddenly, before her eyes, Larry's chest moved, and he took in a long breath of air. He was alive! When the nurse came in and Frances excitedly shared what had happened, he firmly told her, "Don't ever do that again. Let him go!"

Three nights later, on February 8, 1950, the male nurse who had admonished her previously was in the room with Larry. After he made some notes on a chart, he abruptly woke Frances and Tom and said, "He's dead."

Frances was just thirty-three years old. As she listened to the high-pitched trumpet playing taps for her husband, her heart seemed ready to burst. She watched the flag being carefully folded, and each fold was a loud *thud* that tore into her soul. As she and four-year-old Tom stood to receive the flag from Larry's coffin, all she could think was, *My world is over.* Then, she looked at the brave little boy beside her, grasped his hand tightly, and drew herself up to her full height. She decided to face this new challenge and take care of the legacy that Larry had left her—their son.

Grandma Steder

Not long after Larry's death, Frances' mother-in-law decided to move to Florida to be close to her other son and encouraged Frances to come along with her. The two women had a love for each other more like that of a mother and daughter than in-laws. Moreover, Grandma Steder could not stand the thought of being far away from her little "Turtel Taube," the affectionate name she had given to Tom, which is German for "turtledove." She later called him *Hansi*, which means "God is gracious" in German.

Frances wanted Tom to be close to his grandparents, as well, and there was nothing keeping her in Chicago. Not one to let any grass grow under her feet, Frances left Grandma Steder, drove straight home, and hammered a "FOR SALE" sign up in front of her house. Before going inside, she paused and backed into the street to see if the sign was visible from the middle of the road. As she was standing in the street looking at the sign, a car pulled up, and the driver asked if that was her house for sale. A stunned Frances replied, "Yes."

The man and his wife parked their car, walked into the house, and bought it on the spot. Frances thought to herself, *Well, if I had any doubt about whether we should move to Florida, that certainly took care of that!*

A Different World

Housing was much cheaper in Florida than in Chicago, so with Larry's life insurance, Frances was able to pay for a new home in cash.

She was also able to stay at home for a season to raise her son without working at a job. She became active in the local Parent-Teacher Association (PTA), participated in activities with Tom, and joined a nearby Methodist church, which she considered a good way to make contacts.

Frances was able to stay at home for a season to raise her son without working at a job.

People in Frances' neighborhood were easy to meet, outgoing, and close to her age. In the evenings and on weekends, they would gather at each other's houses for neighborhood parties. Frances had never totally abstained from alcohol, but she had consumed liquor only in moderation prior to her move. The neighborhood get-togethers became frequent events, and she found herself enjoying the party atmosphere regularly. On many Saturday nights, she would join a group at the local country club and "dance the night away." Often, she had an excuse not to go to church the next morning because her legs were too sore from dancing. This was the beginning of the Frances whom she would later refer to as "a wild sinner."

A Formidable Challenge

Frances became the life of every party. Her exuberant personality drew friends to her like flies to honey, and she hadn't been in Florida for long before she was introduced to a home builder named Gardner. This was a man who enjoyed a good party and seemed captivated by the young woman who always radiated a zeal for life. He decided that he wanted this woman for a wife, and he knew how to get her.

Any mother with an only son dotes on him and responds warmly to anyone who seems to truly appreciate the many positive attributes of her offspring. Gardner told Frances that he had always wanted a little brown-eyed boy and that Tom was the cutest child he had ever seen. He pointed out Tom's talents and spoke of unlimited potential for his life. He convinced Frances that Tom deserved to have material things now, as well as a future that lacked nothing. When Gardner asked Frances to marry him, she felt something deep inside her shouting "No!" Yet, because she had been persuaded that it would be best for her son, she agreed to the marriage.

Once they had married, Gardner showed his true character. He was an alcoholic who became violent and abusive when intoxicated. The first time he slapped Tom roughly, Frances could not believe her eyes. She threatened to leave if he ever hit Tom again, but the abuse continued whenever he drank.

Frances became pregnant, and her mind would not let her rest. As she went about her daily chores or lay in bed trying to sleep, she dwelled on the thought that she would soon have two children to protect from her husband. She was so stressed that she felt sick and became concerned that her emotional state might harm the baby. She had to get away from her husband.

One evening, Frances tried to leave, but there was nowhere to go. A kind policeman gave her money to stay in a motel for one night with little Tom, but the next morning, she felt like she had no option but to make a humiliating phone call and tell her husband she was going to come back home.

He shouted into the phone, "If you walk into this house, I'm going to shoot you on sight!"

Frances retorted, "If you are going to shoot me, you'll just have to do it because I'm sick and I need a doctor to check me and the baby, and I'm coming home!"

As concerned as Frances was about the effect of months of emotional stress on her pregnancy, a perfect baby girl, Joan Eileen Gardner, was born on June 12, 1953.

Even with a beautiful baby daughter of his own flesh and blood, the man who should have been grateful and loving did not change. The marriage was a battleground. Frances' concern for the safety of her children during her husband's drunken tirades escalated until she knew she had no choice but to leave permanently.

When Joan was four years old, Frances put an escape plan into action. First, she took the children and went to stay with Tom's Grandmother Steder. While staying there, she had a vision in which she saw several people coming to her house and moving her furniture out. One of the people was her husband's best friend. Even though she was not faithful to her church and knew nothing of a personal relationship with Christ, she felt that the vision was from God.

Even though Frances was not faithful to her church and knew nothing of a personal relationship with Christ, she felt that the vision was from God.

Frances called the people she had seen in her vision and asked them to help her move her furniture out while her husband was out of town at a meeting. All the furniture in the house belonged to her, and she was going to need it to furnish a home for her and her children. The people she had called responded and helped her to empty the entire house, except for a bed, a table, and a chair, which she left because she thought that was what the law required.

When Gardner came back to the house and found it almost completely vacant, he was furious. He didn't know how to locate Frances, but he knew how to find out where she would be on a certain day and time.

Frances had organized a Little League baseball club that Tom loved. He never missed a game. Gardner only had to make a phone call to learn when and where Tom's next game would be played. On the day of the game, Frances' intuition told her to take some precautions.

Prior to the game, she told some of the men who had helped her move, "There might be some repercussions because he knows that Tom has a ball game today. If you see his car drive up, please take Joan and run to the clubhouse with her."

"Of course," the men replied.

She then turned to Tom and said, "If you see his car drive up, whatever you're doing, drop your glove and run off the field as fast as you can to the clubhouse!"

Two or three innings into the game, Frances saw the dreaded car appear. The enraged man inside rolled down the window and screamed at the top of his lungs, "I am going to kill you!"

He threw the car door open, lunged out, and strode toward the bleachers where Frances was sitting.

Before he got far, twenty men surrounded him. One father, who was a karate expert, grabbed Gardner from behind and threw him to the ground. In the fall, his ankle snapped. The men picked him up, escorted him back to his car, helped him inside, and shut the door. He drove off, shouting out of the window, "I will get you yet!"

For the next six months, Frances had a police escort wherever she went. When she was driving, a car preceded her, and a car followed her. They stayed with her until the divorce was final. After the court awarded Frances her house, Gardner moved out of the area. There was never again any contact between him and Frances or between him and the children, except for a short and final visit with Joan when she was thirteen.

Frances had never spoken negatively to Joan regarding her father. When Joan was thirteen years old, she told Frances that she would like to visit her daddy because she did not remember him. Even though Frances had realized that it would be natural, one day, for her daughter to want to know more about her father, she wrestled with the question in her heart. To let Joan go was the hardest decision she had ever made.

At the time, Frances' business was small, and she couldn't buy her children all the things she wanted to. So she told Joan, "Your daddy will buy you a wristwatch and some pretty clothes and other things that I may not be able to get for you. I'm going to let you go and visit him for one week, but if you want to come back before the week is over, call me, and I'll make arrangements for you to come home." Joan went to see her father on a Sunday, and she called her mother on Tuesday and asked to come home. That was the last contact anyone in the family had with Gardner.

Back in Business

With two growing children to support, Frances brushed up on her typing skills and started a secretarial service. She had fifteen dollars with which to start her business, and with it she purchased one ream of typing paper, one ream of high quality onionskin paper, and a ream of carbon paper. Her typing skills enabled her to turn out quality work in a short time, and it was not long before she had a number of happy customers.

The tiny office that she rented in exchange for secretarial work quickly grew into a business that was more than Frances could handle alone, so she hired several skilled, reliable girls to work for her. The group of women did such high quality work that they became known as the "Fabulous Females."

The group of women did such high quality work that they became known as the "Fabulous Females."

It became necessary to purchase a mimeograph machine for clients who wanted more than one copy of their documents. In a short time, however, the mimeograph equipment was not enough to keep up with business because of the limited number of quality copies that could be made. Frances was adamant about turning out perfect work for her customers, and she decided that she needed a printing press.

Unfortunately, as Frances related later in life, the printing press taught her to swear. She explained, "The press had sixteen rollers, and when a piece of paper got stuck on the rollers, I had to take the machine apart and clean all sixteen of the rollers with gasoline. That was enough to make you cuss the thing!"

In just a few years, Frances had grown her company from a one-woman typing service to a full-service printing company. She was a successful businesswoman at a time when it was unusual for a woman to own a business. But this was not God's ultimate plan. Soon things would happen that would shake up Frances' world in a way she could not have anticipated.

Chapter Three

Frances Encounters a Living God

With her children growing up in the safe shelter of her love and her printing business more successful than she could have imagined, Frances found that every day nurtured a growing sense of gratitude in her spirit. She did not yet know the "Blesser," but she knew that she was blessed.

A social life was necessary to provide relaxation from the perfectionist demands she placed on herself. Partying was exhilarating, and Frances took advantage of every opportunity to get together with friends and social contacts at cookouts, country clubs, and cocktail parties. In fact, the frequent get-togethers really didn't have life until she arrived. A martini in one hand and a cigarette in the other, she quickly drew a crowd around her to hear her latest round of party jokes. Frances had been larger than average all of her life, and her personality was a perfect fit for her body—abundant and radiating contagious energy.

Frances' vibrant personality, revealing clothes, and exuberance for life attracted men easily, but she steered clear of relationships that might ensnare her or her family. She was responsible, witty, and wise regarding her independence, but she unknowingly fell into the trap of pride and self-sufficiency.

God Dangles the Bait

Young pastor Peter Slagle dropped by Frances' business often to have printing work done for his church. Frances liked him because he was not stiff-necked or religious. After four years of chatting with him on a regular basis and noting that he was always upbeat and nonthreatening, she began to hear what he was patiently planting into her spirit.

"Praise the Lord!" came the greeting as Pastor Slagle poked his head into Frances' office. "I've got some good news! The Lord came through for us again. You know that situation I mentioned last week? God is absolutely faithful to take over when I've just about given up, and I want to tell you that He provided perfect guidance in that matter." The pastor went on to share exciting details of the important breakthrough he had experienced and his sincere gratitude for God's intervention.

Frances had never heard anyone talk about God as if He were a person, much less a friend.

Frances felt her heart rate quicken. Something inside her felt like she had just imbibed a few martinis. She had never heard anyone in her entire life talk about God as if He were a person, much less a friend. She was mystified and curious, and her whole inner being was snapping at the bait.

What is faith? she thought. *What does God do to provide guidance?* Pastor Slagle did not fit into the category of "religious fanatic," which Frances detested. He had something different. Whatever it was, she looked forward to his visits, although she hedged whenever he invited her to church.

"Sorry you can't make it this week, Frances, but I'll be praying for you," Pastor Slagle said as he left, giving her a warm smile. She knew he would do exactly what he said.

A Divine Impact

Excitement was in the air! Frances' little brown-eyed Tom had grown up, seemingly overnight, and had fallen in love. He was married in May 1965. Frances drove to Cocoa Beach to help Tom set up his first apartment. By evening, they had finished moving everything into place, and Frances was driving her new car back home.

The highway was blanketed with thick fog. A young man following Frances strained to see what was ahead of him. Unable to see her vehicle, he crashed his Corvette full force into the rear of her car. The impact was so powerful that her car spun one hundred and eighty degrees, and Frances hit the windshield hard. Wildly cavorting on the black road, the Corvette then struck her car again, and this time, Frances' head hit the window on her left.

At that time, insurance was not required for cars, and when Frances got out of her vehicle to check the damage, she was amazed to find that there was only one little dent in the bumper. She saw no blood anywhere on herself, so she told the other driver, "It's all right. I didn't get hurt and the car didn't get hurt." She felt fine, so she drove home without seeking medical attention.

Three months later, Frances came in from one of her regular Saturday night parties and slipped into bed to read before going to sleep. *What is wrong with this book?* she asked herself. The words simply would not come into focus. She blinked one eye at a time and could not see out of her left eye. Frances removed her glasses to examine them and was surprised to find that the right lens was missing. It had fallen out of the frame and into her handbag. Frances dug around in the bag until she grasped the lens and carefully fitted it back into the frame. How strange that it was the right lens that had fallen out, but her left eye was the one that wasn't working. She lifted her hand to cover her right eye and, to her horror, discovered that her left eye was totally blind!

Frances reasoned, *Oh, well, maybe I had too much to drink. All I need is a good night's sleep, and I'll be back to normal.*

When Frances checked her eyes the following morning, she expected both eyes to be fine, but she panicked when she closed her right eye and saw absolutely nothing. It was a Sunday morning, so she could not contact the optometrist, whose office happened to be right next door to hers.

Frances spent Sunday reading everything she could find about eye problems. When she walked into the optometrist's office the next morning, she told him she had a cataract, and after examining her, he confirmed her self-diagnosis. He sent her to an ophthalmologist, who surprised her by scheduling surgery for Friday morning.

The hospital needed to have Frances checked in by five o'clock on Thursday evening to prepare her for the early morning surgery. Frances told her staff that there was "nothing to it" and to carry on for a few days without her, but inside she was terrified. Before she left the office, she drank martini after martini and puffed cigarette after cigarette until she had numbed her senses enough to proceed to the hospital.

Two hours late and slightly inebriated, she was admitted to her room. As she unpacked her suitcase, she discovered that she had forgotten to bring her Bible. This was the Bible she had been given as a child and it was the only one she had ever owned. She called a friend and asked her to go to the house and bring her Bible to her, explaining that it was precious to her and she couldn't go into surgery without it.

Next, Frances gave her friend instructions on where to find the Bible. It would be on the back of the top shelf in the back bedroom closet. She mentioned that it would probably need to be dusted off because it had been stored there for safekeeping since her last surgery.

When her friend arrived, Frances breathed a long sigh and took her beloved Bible in her hands. She wanted to impress the nurses by appearing to be a very religious person, so she called for them to come into her room. When they had all gathered, she opened her Bible to Psalm 23.

Years before, when she had undergone gall bladder surgery, Frances had read the entire twenty-third psalm. But since eye surgery was a much smaller operation, she decided to read just the first verse: "*The LORD is my shepherd; I shall not want.*" Trying to look very pious, she closed the Bible and lay back on her pillow.

> *"God had dipped His finger in the brilliant red blood of Jesus and had written a very special message just for me."*

The hospital room emptied and, alone with her thoughts, Frances picked up her Bible to read the psalm again. She opened to the page where Psalm 23 had been located just a few moments before, and it was gone! The pages were blank! Incredulous, she watched as words appeared on the pages, written in the brightest red she had ever seen. "God had dipped His finger in the brilliant red blood of Jesus and had written a very special message just for me," she later recalled. "'Frances Gardner' was written on the left-hand side, and on the right-hand side He had written, 'I love you.'"[1]

[1] Frances Hunter, *God Is Fabulous*, revised edition (Kingwood, TX: Hunter Books, 1998), 19.

When Jesus wanted to make a point with His disciples, He spoke in parables. To crowds thirsty for understanding, He explained truths with common analogies that they could comprehend. With Frances Gardner, God used her understanding of printing to speak to her. Frances knew that once a printer's ink is on paper, there is nothing that can remove it. Frances saw, with her one good eye, the printer's ink disappear from two pages of her Bible and the handwriting of God appear in its place. She did not question what she saw.

At that moment, Frances got a glimpse of her life up to that point. Every time she got in trouble, she would say, "God, do this for me," or "God, do that for me." And when the situation was over, she never thought about God again. She said to the Lord, "I promise You this: when I get out of this hospital, I will spend the rest of my life seeing what I can do for You, and not what You can do for me." Without realizing it, she had expressed the secret of Christianity and the foreshadowing of her destiny.

The Dawning of a Destiny

When Frances returned to her room after her surgery, Pastor Slagle was waiting for her. Still not quite coherent, she groggily said to him, "The first place I'm going when I get out of the hospital is to your church."

With surgery behind her and a good prognosis for recovery of her sight, Frances' only challenge was finding colorful eye patches to match all of her outfits. She dove back into her printing business with zeal, but she did not forget her promise to the preacher.

Two weeks after her encounter with God, she walked into Pastor Slagle's church. The young minister preached from John 3:1–3:

> *There was a man of the Pharisees named Nicodemus, a ruler of the Jews. This man came to Jesus by night and said to Him, "Rabbi, we know that You are a teacher come from God; for no one can do these signs that You do unless God is with him." Jesus answered and said to him, "Most assuredly, I say to you, unless one is born again, he cannot see the kingdom of God."*

Frances knew immediately that she had never been born again. Like Nicodemus, she did not understand the concept; her mother had been gone for many years, so how could she be born again?

During the altar call and the "fifty-seven times" the choir sang "Just As I Am," Frances sobbed uncontrollably. She realized for the first time in her life that, even though she always checked the "Christian" box whenever there was a national census, she was not a Christian. She thought to herself, *I can't let God know about this, because He thinks I'm a Christian!*

When the service was finally over, she ran to her car, lit a cigarette, and swore that she would never come back to this dumb church that had made her feel so miserable. But the following Sunday, even though she had intended to go to her seldom-visited Methodist church, it seemed that the car had a mind of its own and ended up right back at the little church. At the altar call, they again sang "Just As I Am," and again she wept. She went straight home, fixed herself a martini, and decided that she would definitely go back to her own church the following week, where she would be safe from "Just As I Am."

For nine months, Frances drove past her old church and returned to Pastor Slagle's church. Although she listened to the sermons and wept at the altar calls with her personal Kleenex box in hand, she still was not exactly sure what she needed to do to have God come into her life.

On a warm February day, Ed Waxer, a representative of Campus Crusade for Christ, pushed open the door to the printing office. He often brought jobs to be printed, so he was not a stranger. This time, he handed Frances a little booklet entitled *The Four Spiritual Laws.* As Ed explained the book and Frances read the simple plan of salvation, everything fell into place. She knew exactly how to be born again and planned what she needed to do.

The next Sunday, February 6, 1966, she went to Pastor Slagle's church, determined that this would be the day she would get saved. She waited for the end of the service and for the choir to start singing "Just As I Am." Instead, they sang "Have Thine own way, Lord; Have Thine own way."

That's not the right song! Frances thought. She waited for them to change over to "Just As I Am," but they didn't. Finally, she decided the song did not matter. She had to go! She stepped out from her seat.

When the church saw that this "wild sinner" was going to the altar, they could not believe their eyes. The power of God was pulsating through the auditorium and, in a few moments, the entire congregation had joined

Frances at the altar, including the pastor. Kneeling and weeping, Frances opened her eyes and realized there was no one to pray for her. So, in her own way of assessing a situation and moving forward, she made a deal with God.

She uttered these words: "God, if You want what's left of this mess, You take me, but You take all of me because I want nothing of myself left!" She continued, "God, I'll make a deal with You—I'll give You *all* of me in exchange for *all* of You."

"God, I'll give You all of me in exchange for all of You."

FIRST STEPS

From the moment Frances left Pastor Slagle's church and drove down Florida Highway 1, she couldn't wait for opportunities to share with others what she had experienced. She stopped at every place that was open along the highway. She did not know how to lead anyone to the Lord at that point, but she didn't have a problem telling everybody that they needed to find Him!

The following Sunday, Frances brought twenty of her friends to church with her—a 50 percent jump in the church's average weekly attendance! Some eyebrows were raised as they walked in because the group consisted of alcoholics, drug addicts, a homosexual, and a prostitute.

The next Sunday, she brought these twenty back plus twenty additional sinners. Some were not even able to walk to the pew—they staggered. In two weeks, the church congregation doubled in size because Frances had exploded with a burning desire to see every single person she came into contact with saved and forgiven by the grace of God. She wanted them to experience the joy of having their burdens lifted as hers had been.

In six months, the little church of forty members had to break ground for a new auditorium because of the number of people from clubs, streets, and neighborhoods whom Frances was bringing to be saved. Then, they had to buy more land to relocate and build an even larger church.

Frances was sensitive not only to souls being led to the kingdom of God, but to the hardworking pastor who led the congregation. She had a nice, large home, and she believed that the pastor and his family deserved a decent home. She told everyone in the church that he was a servant of God and that he needed a house with four bedrooms and a pool for his family. Not everyone was excited, but the new home was built.

Frances demonstrated that it is the responsibility of every Christian to be a bold witness and bring the lost into the kingdom of God.

Frances was just beginning to find out what the Lord can do with a "wild sinner" who is convinced with every fiber of her being that it is not the job of the pastor to get out and do all the work to save the world. She demonstrated with growing passion that it is the responsibility of every Christian to be a bold witness and bring the lost into the kingdom of God.

A Taste of Healing

Long before she was saved, Frances experienced troubling periods of weakness. She would feel sapped of all strength and sometimes would fall asleep while in her chair and slide down onto the floor. Sometimes she would sleep for two or three days at a time. When she was diagnosed with Addison's disease, she was told that the disease can have varied effects on the body, including autoimmune disorders in which the immune system attacks the body's own organs and tissues. Frances' thyroid was affected severely. She was prescribed a dosage of Synthroid so large that it would have killed most people, and she was instructed to take it religiously for the rest of her life or she could die.

The day Frances was saved, she was healed of every symptom of Addison's disease. But she did not know it. No one prayed for her or laid hands on her—she would have thought they were some kind of quack if they had! She had never heard of faith healing, and the little church that was so strong on salvation did not believe that God healed today.

Frances was simply so excited about being saved that she forgot all about the disease. She also forgot about taking her medication. For six months, she was so exuberant that the farthest thing from her mind was taking pills. One day, she suddenly remembered the disease and the medicine that she was never supposed to skip. She realized that she had skipped it for six months! Her first thought was that she was going to die, but the Lord spoke to Frances' spirit, saying that He had taken care of the problem the day she had made the deal with Him. Frances went to her doctor, who pronounced her thyroid completely normal and her body free from Addison's disease!

As if Frances was not already bursting with zeal for the Lord, her gratitude, joy, and adoration for Him escalated beyond containment. Nobody came into her presence without hearing about Jesus!

Money Matters

Until the day she was saved, Frances had never given more than a dollar in a church offering. She would look at the ministers and think, *Money, money, money—that's all they want.* Dutifully, she would reach inside her purse, hoping she would find only dollars and nothing larger, then fold one up neatly and drop it into the offering plate.

When Frances made that trip to the altar and said, "God, I will give You all of me if You will give me all of You," God responded immediately. He said, "The devil has had your money long enough. Now I want it. Give Me 20 percent of everything you've got!"

Frances knew it was the voice of God because she would never have thought of an amount that radical on her own. She was so completely surrendered to God that she obeyed His voice immediately. On the way home, she figured out the value of everything that she owned, including an offer for $100,000 that someone had just made for her printing company. After she tallied up all of her worth, business and personal, she wrote IOUs to God and postdated checks. It took her a year to pay it off, but it taught her about obedience to God, keeping one's word to Him, and something she would one day proclaim everywhere she preached: "You cannot out-give God!"

"You cannot out-give God!"

Consciousness—Not Condemnation

Before Frances was saved, she was not aware that she had any sin in her life. After she was saved, God dealt with her gently, one step at a time, as a loving Father. He instantly delivered her from swearing. From the moment she was saved, no curse word crossed her lips again and no more dirty jokes entered her mind. However, she was not delivered from her bad habits all at once.

Even though she was bringing in the lost from hedges and highways, she had not stopped chain smoking or drinking martinis. God gradually brought those things to her attention. One day, Frances looked around the office and saw cigarette butts everywhere. When she went home, she noticed the smelly ashes in her ashtrays. They suddenly seemed nasty and obnoxious. She began to feel uncomfortable smoking in her pastor's presence.

One evening, Pastor Slagle stopped by the printing office with a small job. Frances had just opened a package from a new carton of cigarettes and lit one up. The second she saw him, she felt guilty and wished she could swallow the cigarette.

"I would quit this stinking habit if I could!" she told him.

He did not lecture her but simply said, "Why don't you ask God to help you?"

She replied, "For a little thing like cigarettes?"

He responded, "A little thing like cigarettes."

She continued, "A stinking thing like cigarettes?"

He echoed, "A stinking thing like cigarettes."

Frances had never realized that God would be interested in little things like cigarettes. She thought He cared only about things like earthquakes and hurricanes. When the pastor left, she cried out, "God, I'm a mess! You know I can't quit. But, God, if I am not presenting my body as a living sacrifice, holy and acceptable to You, please take away this desire."

She turned and put out the cigarette in the ashtray. Later that night, she wrote the date on a little piece of paper, taped it on top of the package of cigarettes, and, at three o'clock in the morning, drove by the pastor's house and tossed the package on his porch. When he came outside the next morning, he knew what had happened! Frances was instantly delivered from her five-pack-a-day habit, and she never put a cigarette into her mouth again. She later became famous for her cigarette-stomping altar calls, where thousands of people were delivered from their smoking habits.

God was gentle on Frances. He dealt first with her need for Him. Then, He dealt with her sins one by one. They had made a deal, after all, and God was ready to give all of Himself to Frances as she gave all of herself to Him.

Frances loved martinis. She liked them dry, so she never put vermouth in her drinks, using only straight gin and olives. She also enjoyed the feeling she had after having a few drinks, although she was never an alcoholic.

Fortunately, Frances' young pastor was wise enough to make no demands on her. He never passed judgment on her or made her feel guilty. He was sensitive to her convictions and pointed her in the right direction. When Frances gave up her martinis, it was not because she felt she that had to do it.

One evening, she was at a friend's house and the girl's husband said, "Well, holy Josephine, I guess you've gotten so pious since you got saved that you won't take a martini anymore."

Frances looked at the martini and didn't know what to do! She wondered if it would be sociable to just pick up the glass and hold it but not drink anything. But she knew that would be a compromise, and God would not honor compromise. She closed her eyes and said, "God, what shall I do?" When she opened her eyes and looked at the martini glass, the martini had turned into a snake, a sign of evil in the Bible.

God said to Frances, as clearly as she had ever heard anything, "Alcohol has no part in your life." She hasn't had a taste of alcohol since that day, and she even refuses to eat food that has been cooked with any type of alcohol.

Frances had an overpowering desire to draw as close to the Lord as she could. She simply wanted more of God, and the more she got of Him, the less she cared about pleasing herself. Frances would later tell multitudes of people that she never gave up drinking, she just changed fountains; she never gave up dancing, she just changed partners.

The Go-Go Girls

Frances' first convert was the "cat burglar" of Miami, who now pastors a large church in Florida. Her second convert was her thirteen-year-old daughter, Joan. Several years later, they were talking about the changes in their lives, and Frances asked Joan, "What made you turn to God so quickly and accept Jesus just one month after Momma did?"

Joan replied, "Because of the change I saw in you!"

Tom took a little longer. He had grown up with a mother who drank, smoked, and swore, and he thought this "Jesus thing" would soon wear off. Eventually, he came to his own conclusion that the God his mother served was real, and he invited Jesus into his life.

The burning desire within Frances to see lives forever changed by Jesus grew so strong that she could think of little else. Ed Waxer, who had given her *The Four Spiritual Laws,* was a regular customer, and one day he brought by a "rush job" and asked if Frances could handle it. She responded that she certainly could—if he would agree to train people in her church on how to use *The Four Spiritual Laws* to lead people to Jesus. Ed was busy activating the Campus Crusade for Christ program in Miami, but he agreed to come to her house and show three of her friends how to use the booklets. Frances invited not just three but seven!

Frances' enthusiasm for winning the lost flowed over onto her church, and a "GO" committee was organized with the assignment to go and knock on doors for Jesus. The church printed "GO" cards with addresses of particular homes where they would present *The Four Spiritual Laws* to whoever lived there.

Frances and her friend Barb became known as the "Go-Go Girls." They promised that they would visit their assigned home and witness to someone before the next Sunday evening service. After coming up with excuses all week long, they found themselves standing in front of the house on Sunday afternoon.

"Oh, please, God, don't let this person be home," prayed Frances and Barb, as they nervously rang the doorbell of the home they were assigned. If no one was home, at least they could go back to church and say that they had tried.

"Hello!" said the woman who opened the door, courteously inviting the two terrified soulwinners inside. By prior agreement, Barb took the lead and read all four spiritual laws to the woman. She then asked her if she would like to ask Jesus to come into her heart, and the woman answered with an enthusiastic "Yes!" Her response nearly knocked them over. In amazement, Barb invited her to pray, and the woman was saved before their eyes.

Frances led scores of people to church to get them saved, but this experience of two ordinary women leading someone to Jesus was the most exciting thing that had happened yet in her walk with the Lord. The "Go-Go Girls" went out again within two days. This time, Frances took the lead, and she was "hooked" forever. She and Barb continued to make house calls and won many to the Lord.

In the Beginning Was the Word...and the Word Was God

Besides leading people to Jesus, Frances' greatest enjoyment came from reading the Word of God. When she fell in love with Jesus, she fell in love with the Bible. She struggled with the King James Version, however, and her pastor assured her it would be all right to read the *Revised Standard Version.*

When Frances fell in love with Jesus, she fell in love with the Bible.

Whenever a new Bible translation was developed, Frances got her hands on it as soon as she could. Her favorites over the course of time narrowed down to *The Living Bible, The Amplified Bible*, and the *New King James Version.* She devoured the Word of God like a person who had been living in a land of famine and had now come into the land of prosperity. In the years that followed, whenever Frances taught on a passage of

Scripture, that selection was always "her very favorite" Scripture, because every single word of God was her favorite.

Her motto became, "If God said it, I believe it, and that settles it." She took God at His word and believed Him. She studied it, memorized it, and applied it. She was in love!

The church she had avoided for many long years became Frances' source of inspiration and illumination. She feasted on the sermons of her pastor and the teaching ministries of the men and women who held meetings anywhere within driving distance. It was as if she had just discovered wells of living water after being in a parched desert all of her life. She drank in the waters and grew spiritually by leaps and bounds. Her character and personality, already well-developed in strength, zeal, love, and determination, became charged with an indescribable power.

Frances was consumed with saving souls. She determined that no one should go to hell, and she was going to do everything in her power to point them in the opposite direction!

She read in her Bible that Jesus instructed His disciples to be witnesses of Him "*in Jerusalem, and in all Judea and Samaria, and to the end of the earth*" (Acts 1:8). Frances began in her family and her social circle, then went into the shopping mall where her printing business was located. She reached out to her neighbors throughout the city of Kendall, a suburb of Miami. Then God laid Miami on her heart. At first, she worried, *If I am reaching out all over Miami, who will reach Kendall?* But God gave her peace that He had others whom He would use in Kendall. Then, He expanded her vision to include the State of Florida in its entirety.

It became apparent to Frances that, if she was going to be traveling all over the place witnessing, she would not be able to run her business successfully. But Jesus was her first love now, not the printing company. She did want to make sure she had heard the Lord, though, so she "threw out a fleece" for confirmation. She told God that if He wanted her to reach out to all of Florida and beyond, He would have to provide the opportunities.

God answered by sending her to speaking engagements across the United States. Frances would have a lifelong love affair with God, giving all of herself to Him and receiving all of Him, plus all He had prepared for her.

Chapter Four

Charles

Before Frances

Palo Pinto County, Texas, was known as the "cradle of the cattle industry" and the gateway to the Old West. It was in this harsh land of sprawling cattle ranches that Charles Edward Hunter came into the world. Born to James Edward and Minnie Foreman Hunter on July 23, 1920, Charles was told by his mother toward the end of her life that on the night of his birth, angels appeared at her bedside. They had handed her a little package and said, "This is your beloved son," and then vanished.

James and Minnie were homesteaders who, like the rugged pioneers who had preceded them, possessed no fear of hard work and persevered through hardship with determined spirits. Charles was the fifth of six children—three boys and three girls.

When Charles was a child, the Hunters moved to a remote area in northern New Mexico and settled in the beautiful Chama River Valley. The family did not have a surplus in material goods, but they loved their independence and cherished their land with its varied terrain, rushing rivers, and bubbling mountain streams. They felt surrounded by the wealth of God.

Life Lesson in the Alfalfa Field

Charles Hunter's family worked together. Each member had vital responsibilities assigned to him as soon as he reached an appropriate age. One of Charles' first jobs was to herd his father's cattle into the meadow to graze. The task entailed more than just turning the animals loose in a fenced area.

An irrigation ditch ran across the pasture, and both banks of the ditch were carpeted with thick grass and clover. Charles' dad and brothers had planted fields of alfalfa next to the clover. Alfalfa was rich in nutrients and would provide the supplemental nutrition the cattle would require along with their hay in the winter. However, if the cows ate the alfalfa when it was still green, and not yet ripe, they would become bloated and would die if they were not treated immediately. Charles' job was to keep the cows out of the alfalfa in the spring and summer.

Charles' father knew that accidents could happen, so he prepared Charles and told him what he should do in the event that any of the cows got into the alfalfa. Charles would need to herd the animals into a corral as quickly as possible and then run them around the corral for an hour or two until they worked the gas out of their systems and the bloating disappeared. The likelihood of the cattle finding a break in the long fence was slim, but they were prone to sticking their heads through the tight barbed wire strands to nibble on the alfalfa. If they were caught right away, no harm was done, but if they grazed unnoticed, they were in danger.

Charles was very conscientious of his responsibility. Watching the cows for long hours in the warm sun was tedious, however, and sometimes he would settle back to rest and unintentionally doze off. His shepherd dog, Ring, helped him with the cows, but when his master napped, Ring would usually curl up next to him and doze, as well.

Occasionally, on a lazy afternoon, Charles would awaken with a start from his nap, jump up to check the cows, and sure enough, find them munching happily on alfalfa, their necks stretching through the wire fence as far as they could get them. Charles and Ring would round them up, head to the corral, and then spend a couple of hours running the bloated animals around in the hot sun.

In his adult years, as Charles taught the principles of God, he would sometimes use the alfalfa field to illustrate the effect of "nibbling on sin."

In his adult years, as Charles taught the principles of God, he would sometimes use the alfalfa field to illustrate the effect of "nibbling on sin." As the cows were threatened with potential death if the alfalfa were not purged from their systems, so "dabbling in sin" could have fatal consequences if not dealt with swiftly.

The Preacher and the Power

Not long after the Hunters settled in New Mexico, a red-headed itinerant Baptist preacher passed through the valley. He preached the fiery gospel that was to change their lives forever.

Charles' mother had demonstrated a longing to know God for as long as Charles could remember. She talked to God all the time but did not know how to be sure that she had been "saved." James, however, was a man totally ungrounded spiritually. He had tended to livestock and farming demands since he could walk and was more accustomed to the rough talk of ranchers and cowboys than he was to religion. Nonetheless, he was a caring man who prized his family and guided them in the ways that he believed would help them to develop a productive life.

When the Hunters knelt at the altar and gave their lives to Jesus, a peace that passed all understanding flowed into Minnie's heart at last. Charles' father felt a presence of God that, because it had been unfamiliar until then, was undeniable. From that time forward, the children would slip out of their beds in the early morning hours and find their parents standing by the potbellied stove, reading the Bible.

There were two areas in James' life that had plagued him for years: cussing and smoking. Before he was saved, he had an extensive vocabulary of curse words. He used swear words as nouns, verbs, adjectives, conjunctions, commas, exclamation points, dashes, and even some special interjections that he invented. Every attitude and description was always accented by an abundance of his choice words.

After James was saved, God cleaned up his mouth. One day, Charles' mother was watching his father take the rim off of a Model T Ford to repair a flat tire. The Ford Motor Company had not engineered a quick and simple way of repairing flats, and it was easy to smash a finger. Charles' dad was really struggling with the tire. Each time he would hurt his finger, he would say, "Aw, shoot!" Considering his history with language, this was quite an achievement, but the improvement was not good enough for his wife. Minnie called out to him, "Poppa, you haven't quit cussin'; you've just changed the words! Now you are 'shoot' cussin'!"

Before he was saved, Charles' father had tried to quit smoking to please his wife. He had laid his pipe down in the house and gone off into the woods for two days and nights with no pipe and tobacco. But when he returned, he still smoked night and day. After he was saved, however, the Spirit of God spoke to him. He felt the Lord was telling him to stop smoking. As a man who respected authority, and with the power of God to help him, he quit smoking permanently.

Growing Up Spiritually

After they were saved, Charles' parents began taking their children to a little Sunday school in the village. One of the activities Charles found most exciting was memorizing Bible verses. He committed John 3:16 to memory, along with the Beatitudes from Jesus' Sermon on the Mount. (See Matthew 5:3–12.) As he practiced and recited the verses over and over, the whole family grew more familiar with God's Word, as did his dog, Ring, and the cows in the pasture.

In particular, Charles thrived on the stories of Jesus. He visualized Jesus healing the blind man, making the lame walk, casting out devils, and raising the dead, and he thought to himself, *If only I had lived during Jesus' lifetime, I would have seen all those things happen!* Charles would have jumped with joy if he had realized that he would see those things happen during his own lifetime, but he would never have believed that it would happen through a couple called the Happy Hunters!

Because of the high altitude of their area in New Mexico, the growing season was short; some crops would grow beautifully but not have time enough to ripen. This was particularly true of tomatoes. The vines would be full of beautiful, large, green tomatoes, but they never ripened to the luscious, deep red fruit that the family had enjoyed in Texas.

On one occasion, some friends who had journeyed to west Texas to harvest apples and pears brought back samples of the fruit for the Hunters. When Charles bit into a fully ripened pear, he thought it was the most wonderful thing he had ever tasted. As the sweet juice ran down his chin and onto his shirt, he felt like he was eating at a king's table. He would teach in later years that just as a delicious fruit or vegetable needs an adequate growing season in order to develop to its fullest potential, a new

Christian also needs to have a full growing season in order to reach his or her God-given potential.

> *Just as a delicious fruit or vegetable needs an adequate growing season in order to develop to its fullest potential, a new Christian also needs to have a full growing season in order to reach his or her God-given potential.*

A Future Accountant

Since Charles' family worked hard for their livelihood, sometimes incurring losses and recovering from them, they were very frugal. Charles appreciated the value of money from an early age. Once, when a carnival came to town, he and his brother, Clyde, put all their money together and came up with a dime's worth of coins. They considered carefully how they would spend and not waste it.

At the carnival, they did and saw everything for free that they could. When they grew hungry at lunchtime, they passed by all the vendors with their expensive foods and small portions. Instead, they took note of a stack of bananas and were able to purchase six large bananas for their dime. Not only did they receive a bargain, but Charles was able to savor his fill of his very first bananas. He long remembered that he would have been denied this blessing if they had been wasteful with their money.

When Charles was twelve, he moved with his family to Abilene, Texas, where his parents operated a peach orchard. One day, when he was thirteen, he and his sister were hoeing weeds from under the peach trees. She announced that she was either going to marry a man from Denver or be an old maid. Where she got her reasoning, Charles did not know, but he did know that he had a high ambition for his life. He informed his sister that he was going to be an accountant and work inside a cool office. He wasn't sure what an accountant was or what one did, but it sounded good. Working in a nice, cool office had to be a lot better than working out in the hot Texas sun.

Both Charles and his sister fulfilled the words that they spoke that day. Charles became an accountant, and his sister married her man from Denver.

Charles never veered from his decision at thirteen to become an accountant. After he graduated from high school, he attended Drawn Business College in Abilene, which was run by Kenneth Copeland's father, A. W. Copeland, and earned his accounting degree. He pursued his accounting education over several years and took the state examination, which he passed, thereby becoming a certified public accountant (CPA). Years after computers with highly developed accounting software were in common use, Charles still compiled annual reports and analysis charts on ledger paper. When his results were compared with the computer printouts, his work was always perfect.

Beyond Sight and Sound

One of Charles' high school experiences made a particularly deep impression on him. His biology teacher had set up a microscope for the students. Charles had never seen such an instrument before. He could hardly wait for his turn to look through the eyepiece and down the long tube. He had no idea what to expect!

Finally, his turn came. Charles had seen rain fall from the sky all his life, but he had never seen the world inside a drop of water. He took a leaf with its tiny veins branching out over its surface and placed it under the microscope. His eyes beheld a structure of tiny cells—building blocks put together by an Architect larger than man.

Next, the teacher placed a single drop of blood on the little glass plate. There was life in the blood! Charles realized there was a dimension to life that could not be seen with the naked eye. He realized there was a spiritual life that also could not be seen with the eye. A desire was birthed in him to experience things beyond the normal realm of the five senses.

Charles realized there was a dimension to life that could not be seen with the naked eye. He realized there was a spiritual life that also could not be seen with the eye.

Many of Charles' impressions were influenced by his family's decision to receive the Lord, by the stories of Jesus that he loved, and by the value he placed upon the Word of God. He always compared and meditated and analyzed. Small things would often speak to him in ways that did not provoke others to give them a second thought.

During his teenage years, Charles became actively involved in his church. At seventeen, he asked Jesus to become his personal Lord and Savior. By age eighteen, he was serving as a youth leader in his denomination in local and state groups. Although he believed that he was saved, Charles did not have a vibrant, personal relationship with Jesus. There was a void in his heart that caused him to realize there was more to be found in his search for God.

God Grants the Desires of the Heart

The same year that Frances' first husband, Larry Steder, enlisted in the navy to fight in World War II, Charles Hunter drove into downtown Houston to enlist with the Army Air Corps (later to be renamed the U.S. Air Force). He went to the recruiting office, but they had too many volunteers, and Charles was turned down. He was disappointed because the army had already notified him that they were going to draft him, and he preferred the Air Corps. A few days later, while driving back to Houston after visiting his mother in Corpus Christi, Charles was stopped by a Texas highway patrol car. The police officer asked, "Are you Charles E. Hunter?"

Charles answered, "Yes, sir, officer. Is there anything wrong?" Charles knew that he had not been speeding and could not think of any reason why a police officer would stop him.

The officer responded, "The U.S. Army Air Corps has accepted you, and they want you to report in at Ellington Field in Houston."

How the officer had managed to identify his car, Charles did not know. All he knew was that he had somehow received the desire of his heart.

After Charles entered the Air Force, he was sent to England. When they asked what his experience was, he answered that he was an accountant. He never determined if they misunderstood him or ignored him, but they assigned him to nail screens onto windows.

While on his tour of duty, he considered three alternatives for his accounting career: join a large CPA firm, work for a major oil company, or

Charles in the U. S. Air Force, 1944.

start his own accounting practice with a CPA friend with whom he had discussed the possibility. His daydreams revealed which one of these options was his first choice: he dreamt of starting his own practice and having the mayor of Houston as a client.

Charles had enlisted as a buck private. In the twenty-one months that he served, he was promoted to captain, likely because they noted his education, his work ethic, and his executive ability. When the war was over, he was in line to be promoted to major if he reenlisted, but he decided to return to Houston and pursue his career as a CPA.

Within a few days of his arrival back in Houston, Charles and his friend Leonard Helvering opened their practice in a dingy two-room suite in an office building in downtown Houston. Through a new acquaintance, who just happened to be the son-in-law of the mayor, Charles' first client was Mayor Holcombe of Houston! The mayor remained Charles' client until he died. After he died, his family gave Charles the mayor's desk, which is still in use at Hunter Ministries.

Charles was determined in every phase of his life to rise early, organize his day for maximum productivity, and use his time wisely.

Consistent with his background of hard work and frugality, Charles was determined in every phase of his life to rise early, organize his day for maximum productivity, and use his time wisely. Rising later than five o'clock in the morning was, to him, a waste of valuable time. He was equally conscientious throughout the day. When others in his firm left for an hour-long lunch break, Charles remained in the office. Since accountants were paid by the hour, he realized that to be gone for an hour was to lose that income.

Charles had the gifts of being highly motivated and a good multitasker. In the midst of obtaining his CPA certification, serving for a tour in the Air Force, and starting his career, he met and fell in love with his first wife, Jeanne. They had met at church, where they both were involved in various activities, and they were married on June 10, 1942. They never became parents, but they enjoyed twenty-seven years of what Charles describes as "nearly perfect" marriage. Considering the absolute perfection required of an accountant, a nearly perfect marriage must have been gloriously near absolute perfection.

A Spiritually Dried-up Prune

Church was a significant priority in the Hunters' lives. They both sang in the choir and were involved in various outreaches and projects. Charles served as the church treasurer for ten years, and he also served on the board of directors. Charles and Jeanne believed strongly in tithing and, to all observers, were powerful examples of Christian faithfulness and moral responsibility. Although they towered spiritually in the eyes of their peers, Charles would later say that during all of that time he was, spiritually speaking, "a dried-up prune."

Although he towered spiritually in the eyes of his peers, Charles was, spiritually speaking, "a dried-up prune."

The value of an analytical mind is a positive quality when evaluating bookkeeping figures and balances. Accountants are ultimately concerned about the bottom line, the final result. If something is wrong in a job they have completed, it will show up in the bottom line of the ledger page, and the accountant will exert his full energy to determine and correct the problem. This attitude, essential in the business of accounting, became a hindrance in other areas of Charles' life.

As successful as he was as both an accountant and a husband, Charles had a habit of pointing critical fingers at other people. In an instant, it seemed like he could spot a problem in a person, inside and outside the walls of the church. Differences or discrepancies stood out to him and concerned him.

"The Baptists can't be right because they believe in eternal security," Charles pointed out in a friendly discourse. "The Methodists can't be right because they don't submerge for baptism." He added that Roman Catholics couldn't be right because...well, he was not sure exactly why, because he did not know much about Roman Catholics, but he knew they were different.

Charles loved the Word of God, but when he read it, he found himself constantly applying the Scriptures to point out other peoples' imperfections. One night, as he was reading, the words of Jesus in Matthew 6:33 stood out to him: *"But seek first the kingdom of God and His righteousness, and all these things shall be added to you."* As he pondered these words, the Spirit of God impressed upon Charles the need to stop worrying about what other people believed and to concentrate on finding out the spiritual truths of God's kingdom.

In December 1967, Charles and Jeanne both felt very clearly that God was leading them to another place of worship. They had talked about changing churches for several years but waited until they believed it was God's timing. They visited several sanctuaries and felt an immediate bond with a large Methodist congregation nearby. Both agreed that this was their church.

After being in a Christian environment for forty years and professing Jesus as his Savior for thirty, Charles often reached a point where God was squarely challenging him to surrender all. Each time, he would hesitate. He felt his reluctance to surrender was saying no to God, but Charles did not really understand what God wanted him to surrender.

In 1968, during the four weeks preceding Easter, the men of the church met at 6:45 a.m. each Wednesday for breakfast, devotions, and prayer at the altar. More than a hundred men gathered each week. After Easter, Charles became a part of a small group of eight who continued to meet for prayer and Bible study.

In May 1968, at age forty-seven, Charles knelt with a dozen other men on the altar of his church. It was 7:10 a.m. With no one coaxing him, no sermon pressuring him, and no inspiring hymn challenging him, Charles Hunter asked God to take his life and his wife's life, totally and without reservation, and make them spiritually what they should be.

Four months after this experience, Charles received his first instructions from the Lord: "Go into My Word and listen to no man, and let Me tell you what I want you to know."

Charles received his first instructions from the Lord: "Go into My Word and listen to no man, and let Me tell you what I want you to know."

Charles received God's instructions as a mandate. His heart responded with a burning desire to learn everything God wanted him to know. When he awoke in the predawn hours, he reached for his Bible. Before he went to sleep, he devoured God's Word. If he awoke at three o'clock in the morning or had a quiet pause in the evening, he opened the Bible and continued to absorb its contents. Being an accountant, Charles kept a record of his time spent in the Word. Within a year, he had spent more than two thousand hours reading and meditating on Scripture—an average of five and a half hours each day. Charles, as well as Jeanne and the others who knew him well, observed a progressive change in his attitudes, desires, and purposes in life.

Surrender and Peace

On November 22, 1968, Charles sat beside his wife as her doctor opened a chart in his hand. "Is it malignant?" was Jeanne's straightforward question. The doctor responded affirmatively.

Jeanne had undergone surgery in June, but she had been given a clean bill of health when the doctors believed they had removed all of the ovarian cancer. As the months passed, she had experienced unusual weight gain. The doctor now explained that she had a rapidly growing mass in her lower abdomen that was inoperable. Her condition was terminal.

In the last six months of Jeanne's life, Charles witnessed a transformation—not only in Jeanne, but also in himself—that was nothing short of miraculous. For Jeanne, the initial impact of her doctor's news was two days of emotional devastation. Fear took hold of her and tried to rob her of the joy she had experienced as both she and Charles totally surrendered their wills to God and progressed in their walks with Him.

Then, she seemed to gather strength from the throne of God. At her request, Charles called their pastor to have him pray for Jeanne. From that point onward, she was never afraid again. In early December, Charles notified his accounting firm that he would have very limited time to work because he wanted to be with his wife during her illness. Whatever God would do, whether it would be complete healing on this earth or healing in going to heaven, they would go through it together.

The Hunters had contacted a woman by the name of Genevieve Parkhurst, whose teachings on healing ministered greatly to them. On March 25, they received her book, *Healing the Whole Person.* Mrs. Parkhurst called them often over the following weeks to pray for and encourage them. After one of her calls, Charles was reading in the quietness of the night when he was startled by a voice so strong that he thought someone was in the room. The voice spoke three words: "Jeanne is healed." Charles went to bed thanking and praising God for Jeanne's healing.

At about three o'clock in the morning, Charles stirred, stretched quietly, then lay awake in meditation and joyful thanksgiving to God. He later presumed that he had had a vision, for suddenly, he saw his body floating about eighteen inches above his physical body, and the spiritual body started rising. Then he saw Mrs. Parkhurst, whom he had never met in person. She had her hands under his back and was lifting him until he was as high as her arms could reach, and then he kept rising higher and higher. From the time the vision had started, he experienced a series of impulses somewhat like sound waves flowing through his body.

Charles believed that what had happened was the result of Mrs. Parkhurst's lifting him up in prayer before God. He did not see Jesus during this experience, but he felt Him as though He were physically there beside him. As he watched himself descend, the pulsating waves lessened until the experience ended.

Jeanne went to be with the Lord on May 23, 1969. As the spirit of God had told Charles, she was complete and whole—perfectly healed.

Charles wrote of his and Jeanne's spiritual growth during that final year in a book entitled *A Tribute to God.* In it, he said,

> Particularly the last six months of her life, although her health had rapidly waned and extreme weakness, fatigue, and fever plagued her, she attained a faith in God—a faith far greater than any I have ever seen—and approached eternity with such an eager, positive assurance that there was absolutely no room for doubt that she was personally, literally, a child of God going to her eternal home joyfully.[2]

Charles did not realize it at the time, but friends, business associates, and church members were all being influenced spiritually during that final year of Jeanne's life. What could have been a year of demonstrating fear, depression, or anger became for him and his wife a year of exhibiting a release of all their cares and trusting God to do things His way.

After Jeanne went to be with Jesus, Charles experienced only one instance of disturbing grief. For about twenty minutes, he incurred what he described as "the most horrible, lonely, heavy, dark, grief-stricken period I had ever experienced."[3] He asked God to take the heaviness away, if it was from the devil, and to draw near to him. Instantly, the depression left and he was never again visited with loneliness or grief.

---

[2] Charles Hunter, *A Tribute to God* (Kingwood, TX: Hunter Books, 2008), 46.

[3] Ibid., 48.

Chapter Five

Souls, Books, and Suitcases

Word traveled fast in Kendall, Florida, that a woman who used to be a wild sinner had become a Christian with wild enthusiasm, and that she was filling up her church with sinners from all over the place. A church in Homestead, Florida, heard about Frances. When the pastor's office called and asked if she would come and preach, Frances agreed, but she was a nervous wreck.

Her thoughts whirled, *I'm not a preacher! I love to talk to people about Jesus in a personal setting, but what in the world will I say to a church filled with people who have all probably known the Lord a lot longer than I have?*

She decided to go to the only person she knew who could give her advice—her pastor. He told her to read a verse or passage of Scripture, divide it into three points, bring the people to tears with a sad story, and then give them an invitation to receive Christ.

Frances went to Homestead and followed his advice to the letter. When she asked for anyone who wanted prayer to come forward, she was shocked to find that people responded to her invitation. She didn't know what to do or what to say to the people who came. When the first woman said, "My mother is sick," Frances replied, "I'll pray for her as soon as I get home."

As she drove her car back to Kendall, Frances talked with God as she would her best friend. She asked Him, "God, are You sure You called me to be a preacher?"

Frances was called "to be an enthuser, someone to remind people that Jesus Christ is the most exciting Man who ever lived."

God said, "I never called you to be a preacher; I called you to be an enthuser, someone to remind people that Jesus Christ is the most exciting Man who ever lived."

Relieved, Frances assured the Lord that she would be faithful to her unique calling and would never again give a talk like the one in Homestead. She never broke that promise.

From the Pew to the Pulpit

Invitations began to flow to Frances from all over south Florida. In the beginning, the churches she visited were primarily in the non-Pentecostal Church of God denomination in which she had been saved. Although the Church of God did not ordain women, much less divorced ones, they invited Frances to come and minister.

She was an unusual speaker. Once people heard her in one church, they told everyone they knew about her, and then she would get a call from another church. As her reputation grew, she was invited to speak at churches outside her denomination.

People were drawn to Frances because they felt that if this woman could have such an amazing encounter with God, maybe they could, too. They needed to meet a God who loved them. They needed acceptance, hope, and restoration.

But there was something else Frances conveyed in her own unique way. Few people, even if they were saved, had experienced a God they considered personal and exciting. When they heard Frances, something inside their spirits leaped with joy. For too long, they had been dolefully encouraged that if they could just hold on, the Lord would get them through this sorrowful life, and then they would be gloriously happy in heaven. Frances told them that life with God was incredible and that they could be happy right now!

There was talk at times about something that Frances refused to change: she wore makeup and jewelry without apology. Particularly in the Church of God, both men and women were expected to limit jewelry to their wedding bands. Makeup was considered taboo by many denominations. Whenever someone addressed Frances with criticism or a suggestion regarding her appearance, she would answer that when Jesus told her to take off her makeup and jewelry, she would do so; but until then, she would continue to wear them. The only thing the Lord told her to discontinue was nail polish, and she didn't ask why, she just stopped painting her nails.

Heaven must have thundered its applause whenever Frances gave an altar call, because the response of the people was overwhelming. Some churches had experienced only a few souls being saved in the entire life of the church. Frequently, after Frances spoke, a third, a half, or three fourths of the congregation would step forward to receive Christ, often including deacons, choir members, or even the pastor and his wife.

Although Frances was frequently out of town on weekends, when she was home, she was faithful to attend her home church. One Sunday morning after the Sunday school class, she told her pastor that the class was one of the most boring things she had ever sat through. With a twinkle in his eye, he suggested that if she didn't like the class, she should start one of her own!

Always up for a challenge, Frances jumped at the opportunity to start her own Sunday school class. She went to a local Christian bookstore, purchased a book that she thought would be a great one to use for a lesson guide, and started her class the following Sunday morning. Each Saturday that she was in town, she would go back to the bookstore and purchase enough books for everyone in the class. The next morning, with books in everybody's hands, she would take them through her lesson. It was not a surprise when her class became the largest in the church.

Should I Bother You, God?

One day, as Frances was reading her Bible, the page became blurry, causing a sick feeling to rise in her stomach. *Maybe it's these glasses,* she thought.

She removed her eyeglasses and examined them. Without her glasses on, she couldn't see whether there were any smudges on the lenses, so she cleaned them just to be sure and put them back on. There was no change. She squinted but couldn't tell if that helped or not. Then, she closed her right eye to test the left eye, which had undergone the cataract surgery a year earlier. "Hmmm, nothing wrong there," she muttered. "Let's try the other one."

She took a long breath and covered her left eye. After she had gazed at her Bible for a few seconds, she made an appointment with her ophthalmologist.

Frances sat silently in the doctor's office and listened to the ophthalmologist as he told her that if she did not have surgery, she would lose vision completely in her right eye—her "good" eye! If she did have surgery, she would be totally blind for at least two months while recovering. Even then, there was no guarantee as to the long-term results.

As Frances drove home, she debated whether to ask God to heal her or not. She had never heard anyone teach on healing. Her church did not tell people to believe in the healing power of God. She knew that God could heal if He wanted to—after all, her Addison's disease had gone away, and she hadn't even asked Him. She wondered if healing came now and then to people when it was God's idea, or if He would heal when someone actually asked Him. She didn't want to be selfish. When she finally arrived home, she had decided that she wouldn't ask God for healing directly, but that she would commit the entire situation to the Lord and not bother Him about it any further.

As time went on, her eyesight grew progressively worse. It became difficult to drive safely in the daytime and impossible to do so at night. She grew uneasy picking up people to take to church, and if she returned them home at night, it was a true act of faith by everyone concerned.

One Sunday, Pastor Slagle preached a message that released Frances to feel confident in asking God to heal her eye. All week long, she continued to ask Him to heal her eye. She wondered if she should keep asking or if one time was enough. Was she showing a lack of faith if she continued to ask?

At the end of the week, Frances took her copy of *Living Letters* (forerunner to *The Living Bible*) to her Saturday hair appointment. She opened it to Ephesians 6:18 and read, *"Pray all the time. Ask God for anything in line with the Holy Spirit's wishes. Plead with him, reminding him of your needs"* (TLB).

She began to pray harder than she had prayed for anything else in her life. She pleaded earnestly with God about the situation. While she was sitting in the beauty parlor, God reached down and touched her eye. She had her eyes closed while she prayed, but she knew before she opened them that her eye had been healed.

An overwhelming sense of awe and gratitude for the goodness of God filled Frances from the top of her head to the tips of her toes. Frances did not have any faith for healing. She had never heard a sermon on confessing God's Word. She just knew, for sure, that God could do anything.

Frances had never heard a sermon on confessing God's Word. She just knew, for sure, that God could do anything.

The One and the Many

When Frances began her speaking engagements all over Florida, she did not give up her passion for personal soulwinning. Each evening, she and her daughter, Joan, would visit three homes. Joan went along as a babysitter for the small children so that Frances could speak to the adults and older children.

Frances would knock on the door and, since people did not feel as threatened by strangers in those days, the resident would usually invite the mother and daughter to come inside. Frances would make small talk with them until she sensed the point of their spiritual need. Then, she would bring out The Four Spiritual Laws booklet and walk them through the four steps to receiving Christ. Next, she would have them repeat the sinner's prayer.

By the end of her visit, people felt they had known Frances for a lifetime, and when she invited them to come to her church on Sunday, they did not feel uncomfortable responding to her invitation. The church grew, and her Sunday school class overflowed!

God Is Fabulous

Something was moving in Frances' spirit. She couldn't get away from it whether she was driving, cooking, or brushing her teeth. Any time she was not totally enveloped in work, church, or ministering, she found herself thinking, How in the world can I ever preach God's incredible love to everybody on this planet? There are only so many places I can be at one time. In fact, I can only be at one place at a time!

She looked at the machine in front of her. The burden to share her testimony had grown until she knew that it had to be from God and that she needed to obey. The office had closed for the day. Alone in the quiet, Frances placed a piece of paper in the typewriter and began to type, "I became a Christian at the age of forty-nine." Then, her mind went blank.

The next night, after everyone had left the office, she sat down again, arranged her fresh sheet of paper, and typed, "When I was forty-nine, I became a Christian." Nothing else came to her mind. She continued to do this night after night. No matter how hard she tried, she could get no farther than different versions of, "I found Jesus Christ when I was forty-nine."

Frances shared with Pastor Slagle her frustrating attempts to put her testimony into writing. He gave her advice that she applied not just to her first book, but also to the many which have been written since then: "Frances, go back to your typewriter and pray, asking the Holy Spirit to give you the words."

With the printing office again locked and silent, Frances settled into her chair. She prayed the way her pastor had instructed: "Father, may Your Holy Spirit direct my fingers and my brain. Please use them to write the story that You want written. In Jesus' name, amen."

She inserted a sheet of paper, turned the carriage until just enough margin appeared, and began. God had already quickened several Scriptures to her. Rapidly, the words of John 10:10, Romans 3:23, and Ephesians 2:8–9 appeared on the page. Her thoughts began to flow effortlessly, and before she knew it, she needed to insert a clean sheet of paper. The following words appeared:

> Church honestly bored me, and my most awful thoughts came to me while sitting in church. Obviously, I wasn't listening in spite of my so-called Christianity, so I began to find excuses for not attending church. After a few years, I didn't even find it necessary to make excuses for not going to church....
>
> But God has an interesting way of dealing with people like me. I shall always feel that God loved me very much because he really

went out of his way to bring me into his fold. I wonder if any maverick was ever broken who kicked as hard and as long as I did.[4]

The book was almost developing more rapidly than her 125-words-per-minute rate could type it. It was as if her fingers had little brains in them. Her first book, God Is Fabulous, was written in the next thirty hours. She never rewrote or edited it. The publisher changed fewer than ten words. Her next book, Go, Man, Go, a book about witnessing, was written in the same way, flowing out of her with no editing or rewriting. Frances never felt that she should take credit for the books that she wrote, and she gave all the glory to the God who anointed her brain and fingers.

Frances never felt that she should take credit for the books that she wrote, and she gave all the glory to the God who anointed her brain and fingers.

The High Calling of Christ

"Gene Cotton, you have an absolutely incredible talent!" exclaimed Frances at her dining room table. "But there is no way I can be your manager," she continued. "I just don't know anything about music, show business, or bookings."

Frances told Gene she would pray earnestly about his request, then hung up the phone. She decided to ask God to indicate to her if it was His will for her to be Gene's manager. She opened her Bible, and two verses from Romans stood out.

For I long to see you, that I may impart to you some spiritual gift, so that you may be established; that is, that I may be encouraged together with you by the mutual faith both of you and me.

(Romans 1:11–12)

Frances felt a surge of peace about helping Gene as his manager. She immediately took a plane to New York and signed a contract with him.

The next evening, Gene was scheduled for an audition in a coffeehouse. They prayed about what songs he should sing and what instruments he should play, and they agreed on four songs.

[4] Frances Gardner, *God Is Fabulous* (Anderson, IN: Warner Press, 1968), 13.

As Gene prepared to go onstage, Frances went to the ladies' room to straighten her hair and powder her nose. When she walked back, the lights had been turned down, and she could not see the deep step in front of her. The heel of her shoe caught on the edge of the step, and she tumbled violently to the floor. People came from everywhere to help her up. In a muffled voice, so as not to disturb anyone, she told them, "My foot is broken."

Her foot was throbbing. She could see it swelling and changing color before her eyes. But she did not want to upset Gene before he sang, so she remained seated on the floor while he performed all four songs. As Frances listened intently, thinking what a beautiful voice he had and what a bright future lay before him, she felt a piercing stab in her spirit. She realized that not one song they had picked mentioned faith or would turn anyone's attention to the Lord. They had left God out of the audition.

Gene helped her back to the dingy Greenwich Village hotel room that he had reserved for her, since he and his friends were staying there. They spent hours transferring her foot from hot to cold water, but the pain increased so intensely that they decided to take her to the hospital.

The hotel room seemed to be a mile from the elevator. Frances could not put any pressure on her foot, so they clasped their hands under her and carried her. When they finally arrived in the lobby, the hotel clerk offered to call for an ambulance, but a serious subway accident had left no ambulances available. They decided their best bet was to get a taxi, so they went outside, but no taxis were in sight.

Her young friends propped Frances up against a lamppost and went looking for a cab. Frances wondered what her church would think if they could see her in New York City in the middle of the night, leaning against a lamppost, teetering precariously on her good foot while the other pulsated with pain.

As she stood there with one shoe on and one shoe off, looking as if she would fall down at any moment, a police car pulled up to the curb beside her. The officer rolled down the window and asked if she was all right. Informed of her plight, he arranged for a cab to pick her up and for someone at the hospital to meet her at the door with a wheelchair.

"This foot is broken in three places," the X-ray technician told Frances.

"We will have an orthopedic surgeon come and set your foot properly. Just sit tight. He isn't in the building, but we're calling him now."

At five o'clock in the morning, a nurse approached Frances and told her that the surgeon was not going to be able to come. They would have someone dress the foot as best he could and release her.

The tired group returned to the hotel. All night long, Frances had been searching her heart. Why had this happened? She grew convinced that she had walked out of God's protection because she, the manager for a young Christian singer, had not influenced him to sing at least one song in his audition that would glorify God. She later told Gene that, as long as she had anything to do with his career in the future, he would always sing at least one spiritual song, regardless of the audience.

This was a "Gethsemane experience" for Frances. She spent the next day in bed with her Bible before her, calling out to God with a broken and contrite heart. "Father, in Jesus' name, I ask You to forgive me for this stupid sin of not putting You entirely first. I promise You that I will never do anything like this again as long as I live. Please heal this foot, God, so I can get back to doing the things You have called me to do."

Frances continued to entreat the Lord until Gene and the others arrived to take her back to the hospital. The moment Gene laid eyes on Frances, he knew God had done something during the day.

Once at the hospital, Frances refused treatment. She told them, "I'm going back home because I want the doctor who sets my foot to be nearby in case I run into trouble." With that being said, she signed a release form and left.

The young men helped Frances into a taxicab, piling her crutches, foot dressings, and luggage in the trunk. The New York cab driver raced through the streets to the airport because it was getting dangerously close to the time of Frances' plane was scheduled to depart. When they got to the airport, Gene rushed ahead, and Frances threw caution to the wind and began to run to catch the plane, forgetting about her broken foot.

As Frances went down the ramp to catch the waiting plane, Gene noticed with amazement that Frances was now limping on the wrong foot. He mentioned it to her, and without skipping a step, Frances responded, "I know it! The Great Physician has healed my foot!" Today, when she tells the story of that healing, Frances says, "When I remembered that I was supposed to be limping, I didn't think about which foot."

Once back in Florida, Frances had new X-rays taken of her foot. The doctor who read them confirmed what she already knew: not one bone was broken.

There is absolutely nothing God won't do when His child has a contrite and humble spirit.

Frances looked back on this experience as a powerful tool that God had used to teach her His will on total surrender, absolute obedience, and uninterrupted faithfulness. The high calling on her life would require much on her part. But she also learned that there is absolutely nothing God won't do when His child has a contrite and humble spirit.

Rewards for God's Faithful Enthuser

In the summer of 1967, Frances attended the annual Church of God camp meeting in Anderson, Indiana, an event that attracted thousands of attendees each year. Frances anticipated an inspiring week of spiritual feasts in God's Word. She left the meeting totally disappointed. She felt like they had all been trying to see who could make the biggest impression from the pulpit. Even though she knew the Church of God's policy on women ministers, she prayed that God would make a way for her to be a speaker there the following year. She believed that she had something to share that would fire them up!

Frances at her first autograph party with her book *God Is Fabulous.*

By the next year, Warner Press had published her book *God Is Fabulous,* and it had become an immediate national best seller. Much to Frances' delight, she received an invitation from the Church of God to speak at the 1968 national camp meeting!

The big week finally arrived, and on the day Frances was to minister, the situation was not as positive as she would have liked. Not everyone was excited that she was on the lineup of speakers. A group of men expressed their offense at a woman speaker by boycotting the service. They gathered together at the entrance of Warner Auditorium to voice their disapproval and refused to go inside.

When Frances began her message, she had no notes or outlines. It was her custom to speak from her heart, and she told how God had transformed her life from a wild sinner to a wild soulwinner. She described an exciting God who had forgiven her, cleaned her up, and filled her with a passion and energy to convey His love to everybody she met. Her relationship with God was more real, more intimate, and more rewarding than even her relationships with her children.

Each camp meeting speaker was limited to fifty-eight minutes for his or her presentation. When Frances glanced at her watch and saw that she had talked for fifty-seven minutes, she knew that it was time to stop or somebody would stop her.

She placed her head on the pulpit and closed with a prayer. "God, may I have been the woman You called me to be. May I have said what You told me to say."

She did not look up from the pulpit. She wasn't sure if the crowd of five thousand had heard anything she had said. She was near tears, knowing that she had so much in her heart to convey but not knowing if the people had heard the cry of her soul.

Suddenly, the sound of a mighty wind filled the building. Frances thought it was the bustling motion of the crowd starting to leave. She lifted her eyes to see people all over the auditorium rising from their seats and coming forward. Men and women were weeping under the influence of the Holy Spirit's presence. They pressed forward as if the Lord Himself were at the front and their eternal salvation depended upon their getting to the altar.

Three thousand people jammed the aisles and pushed their way up front in response to the woman preacher who had given her life completely over to God. They saw that she was not playing church; she was in love with Jesus, and she was passionate about sharing Him with the world around her. A large proportion of those who came forward were pastors, deacons, board members, and their wives. They accepted Frances' challenge to make a difference in their churches and throughout the world. Her pastor went back to the pulpit and told them to stop coming because there wasn't room for anybody else.

> *Three thousand people saw that she was in love with Jesus, and she was passionate about sharing Him with the world around her.*

Harold Phillips, an editor with Warner Press, ran to the men who had boycotted the service, shouting, "The Holy Spirit has fallen on Warner Auditorium! The Holy Spirit has fallen on Warner Auditorium!" This very proper denominational leader was totally disheveled, his shirttails flying in the breeze as he ran.

The Church of God denomination was turned upside down in one afternoon. Those who had been making their narrow-minded statement on the outside had missed it!

Frances began to receive more speaking invitations than she could fulfill. A growing number of calls came from churches outside her denomination. She kept her bags packed, unpacking them just to wash her clothes and repack them for the next trip. Burning with a passion to tell everyone on the planet about Jesus, she was content to remain single and travel everywhere by herself for the God she served.

Among the people who heard the exciting reports of the Church of God camp meeting was a tall, handsome accountant who had been recently widowed. He had not been at the event, but after hearing his brother's account of the move of God that shook Warner Auditorium, he determined to hear in person this exuberant woman who was on fire for God.

Chapter Six

A Divine Love Affair

Charles Hunter had been given a little book with a vivid pink cover entitled *God Is Fabulous*. He read, with tears and laughter, the account of a Miami businesswoman whose life had been radically changed by a personal encounter with a living God. Soon afterward, he heard reports that an entire denomination was talking about the woman preacher who had shaken things up at their annual camp meeting. Charles made up his mind to meet Frances Gardner.

Charles found out that Frances was going to be in Houston during the first week of October to speak at a college affiliated with the Church of God. He decided to call her in Florida and invite her to stay at his home while she was ministering.

Frances had discovered something very interesting: pastors think that they have a second calling in matchmaking. The pastor of each church she spoke at would often have people over to his home for something to eat after the service. Since Frances was a single woman speaking around the nation, each pastor usually left an empty chair beside her for the church's most eligible bachelor. Each pastor was hoping that Frances would fall in love with that church member, marry him, and then help build the church the way she had built the one in Kendall.

When Charles called Frances for the first time and her secretary told her that a man named Charles Hunter had called, she responded, "Some nut! Just like the rest of them!" and did not return the call.

Frances and her daughter went out the next night to win people to Jesus, and while they were away, a second call from Charles came in. When she came back and heard that he had called again, she said, "He is still some nut! He's probably just a little more persistent."

When she went out the third night and came back, her secretary said, "That Mr. Hunter called again, and I think you ought to call him, because he sounded so nice."

Frances thought he was just more persistent than the rest of them, but for some reason, she decided to dial his number. In Houston, Charles picked up the receiver.

"God is fabulous! This is Frances Gardner," Frances dutifully identified herself. She had just returned to the office and was absorbed in proofing some of the material that the night shift was printing for her, so she was not listening very attentively to what Mr. Hunter said.

Charles explained, "I just learned that you will be speaking for a week here in Houston. I have been working with youth at our church, and I'd like to invite you to speak to them, if your schedule permits. I have a large home. My wife died, and I have a Christian housekeeper. I would love for you to stay here while you are in Houston. I will go and stay in a local motel."

That is not what Frances heard; the only words she heard him say were, "I would like for you to come and stay at my house." With that, she hung up and left Charles in absolute silence.

Frances turned to her secretary, and the first thing she said about the man who would become her beloved husband was, "That dirty old man! Who does he think he is, and who does he think I am? He wanted me to come and stay at his house!"

While Frances indignantly told her secretary about a "dirty old man" who wanted her to stay at his house in Houston, Charles pursued his goal with even more resolve than he had felt before their brief conversation.

Frances left Florida and ministered in Oklahoma before heading to Houston, where she was anxious to minister to the students. Her first stop was at the office of the college president to pick up her two-page schedule. Pleased to see that she was going to be so busy, her eyes widened and her mouth dropped open when she spotted the name "Charles Hunter" on the second page. She thought to herself, *Wait until I meet him; I'll freeze him out!*

She had her opportunity at the end of the week when she walked into the church where she was to speak that night. The pastor greeted her with, "I have someone special I'd like you to meet!" He paused as Frances smiled and extended her hand. "This is Charles Hunter."

A Cold Reception

Frances' smile vanished, and she gave Charles an icy stare and a stiff, unwelcoming handshake. However, the instant their hands met, she felt what she could describe only as the "hot, electrical power of the Holy Spirit" in his touch. She was speechless.

> *The instant their hands met, Frances felt what she could describe only as the "hot, electrical power of the Holy Spirit" in Charles' touch.*

Charles looked at Frances with the most sincere smile she had ever seen in her life. Neither said a word, but they both stood there, oblivious of the pastor's presence, for at least two minutes. Finally, Frances looked down to see what Charles was holding in his hand and realized it was her hand still in his. She pulled her hand away and placed it behind her back, then left to participate in the service.

The next morning, Frances addressed the students at a prayer breakfast. As her eyes scanned the attentive group before her, she noticed that Charles Hunter was present. When the meeting concluded, she spoke to him, but only to tell him the time and place to pick her up the following morning so that she could address his youth group.

When Charles arrived the next day, he greeted Frances with that same penetrating smile and gently took her arm to walk her to his car. He opened the door and made certain she was seated comfortably before closing it. Once they were on the road, it did not take him long to convince her that he was not the "dirty old man" she had initially imagined. He gave his testimony, describing himself as a spiritual "dried-up prune" for over thirty years. He told Frances how the Lord had moved in his and his wife's lives to become a real and living force that had propelled them both over the months of her illness and death.

Frances listened intently. She identified with everything he told her. In fact, she felt an immediate and strong connection with him.

She ministered to the youth in Charles' church and spoke at another church that evening. Afterward, she remembered that she had promised to see some friends while in Houston. Although it was nearly eleven o'clock when Frances finished speaking, she announced that she needed to get to a certain address to meet some friends from Campus Crusade for Christ and asked if anyone was available to take her.

The crowd parted like the Red Sea, and walking down through the opening was Charles Hunter. He assured her that he was available to take her anywhere she wanted to go. When they arrived at the address, the couple greeted them joyfully, even though they had been asleep, and the next three hours seemed to be just a few minutes because of the exciting testimony that each person shared.

At two o'clock in the morning, Charles returned Frances to the student's apartment that she had used for the week. Before going inside, Frances said, "I never end a night without prayer, so would you like to pray with me?"

Charles reached over and took her hand, and they prayed. When they had finished praying, he opened his wallet, took out a small card, and stuck it in her purse. He said, "I want to give you my business card, because if you are ever anywhere in the whole world and you need something, call me, and if it is possible, I will see that you get it."

Then, instead of leaving, Charles asked Frances to pray with him about a friend of his. The two of them clasped hands and prayed. Then, Charles placed a second business card into her purse.

In Frances' recollection, "at least twenty-seven prayers and twenty-seven business cards later," Charles reluctantly turned to leave. But, before he left, he reminded Frances that if she ever needed anything, wherever she was, to contact him and he would make sure she got what she needed, if it was possible.

Back in Florida

The next morning, the president of the college took Frances to the airport. As the big jet took off, she looked out the window and secretly wondered which building Charles was in. She was startled to notice her heart racing as she thought of him. She told herself, *Enough of that! God has put a call on my life, and I don't have time for things like romance.*

Frances was startled to notice her heart racing as she thought of Charles.

On October 9, 1969, Frances had barely unpacked her suitcases from the Houston trip when she felt compelled to write a letter to Charles. Due to her hectic travel schedule, she was normally not a letter writer and used the phone for communicating. But she wanted to thank him properly for the generous check he had personally given her for speaking at his church's youth group. It was the largest check ever given to her ministry.

The next morning, she sat down and wrote a second letter. She was amazed with herself that she had written the letters, but she felt as though she had known Charles all her life. She believed that he was genuinely interested in what was happening in her life, and she wanted to share everything with him. In the second letter, she invited him to attend a New Year's Eve party at her church. She had not been on a date in many years, and this was not really a date, but she somehow felt comfortable asking a man to travel twelve hundred miles to attend a party for just a few hours.

Charles wrote a very long letter in reply to Frances's invitation. He told her many things, detailing all of his activities as though he were talking with her in person. He had purchased fifty of her books to give away. He had paid for two thousand of *The Four Spiritual Laws* booklets and sent them to the Gulf Coast Bible College. He wrote and wrote and shared and shared. Finally, he mentioned that, "Yes," he would love to come to the New Year's Eve party at her church!

Houston's Most Eligible Bachelor

Charles and Frances fell into a routine of phone calls and letters. Frances typed her letters because, as she told Charles, her handwriting was illegible, and she could say much more in typing because she typed 125 words per minute. Charles handwrote his letters in what Frances described as "beautiful penmanship." The letters were full of the events of their lives. They wrote about books they were reading and Bible verses that spoke to them. Frances shared details of her travels and services where she ministered. Charles was still very much involved in his local church and described the various ways the Lord was using him, as well as how He was touching his own life.

Frances found herself irresistibly drawn to this gentle man with quiet strength. He was obviously on fire for God. She had a desire to share everything with him, but she knew beyond the shadow of a doubt that God had a special calling on her life. Given the significant amount of time she was spending thinking about Charles, writing to him, and talking to him on the phone, she figured that either the devil had sent him to distract her or he was sent from God to help her. One night, Frances prayed, "God, if Charles is not of You, let him fall in love with someone else before he comes to Miami." Then she cried all night. She knew she wanted Charles, but she also knew that if Charles was not of God, she did not want him.

Whether by coincidence or not, Charles suddenly became the most eligible bachelor in Houston.

Whether by coincidence or not, Charles suddenly became the most eligible bachelor in Houston. He was flooded with invitations to dinner parties and functions of various kinds. Most of the invitations were from very attractive women—all the right age, and all very eligible. Charles knew nothing of Frances' conversation with God about him. He was bewildered by the sudden surge in attention. He later told Frances that all of these women were ladies with spiritual problems who could see the change in his life and wanted this same excitement in their own lives. To help them, Charles would give them copies of Frances' books. He would then tell them that he had to cut their "date" short so that he could call Frances at eleven o'clock Houston time, midnight in Miami. He was not interested in attracting any of the women.

Scriptural Preparation

By mid-November, Frances had completed another book, *Hot Line to Heaven.* When she completed the manuscript, she sent a copy to Charles. After he received it, he mentioned that he had given his mother a copy of her first book. He told Frances that he had also hinted to his parents of a budding relationship between him and the author of the book. They were looking forward to meeting her!

Frances' intuition made her heart leap, even though the topics of love and marriage had never entered any of their communication. After talking to him for nearly an hour on the night of November 25, Frances awoke from a sound sleep at 1:30 in the morning. She got her Bible and began to search the Old Testament for a certain passage. God urged her to memorize two verses that would be the answer to Charles when he asked her to marry him.

When she found the verses, Frances went to her typewriter and typed these words in a note to Charles: "I was utterly compelled to search out a verse of Scripture and memorize it (actually two). In God's perfect timing, I'll tell you the verses. In the meantime, please hold this in your wallet."

Mother Has a Crush on Mr. Hunter

Joan had never met Charles in person, but she was very aware that her mother rushed home every night so as not to miss her phone calls from Charles. Sometimes, Joan would get to the phone before her mother and have a short conversation with Charles. She would then tease her mother as only a teenager can, "My mother is fifty-three and has a crush on a man she doesn't even know!" One night, she told Frances, "Mom, I wish you'd marry this Charles Hunter."

Frances quickly retorted, "Joan, get that right out of your mind this instant. You know I'm going to have a mad, wild love affair with God the rest of my life, and there isn't any possible way I could ever think of marrying and still run around the country doing what God has called me to do."

Joan shrugged her shoulders and replied, "Well, I still think it would be cool if you married him."

Joan entered the hospital on the first of December to have ear surgery. The surgery turned out to be more complex than initially expected, and Joan was under the influence of the anesthesia for most of the day. About noon, a dozen long stemmed red roses arrived in her hospital room, along with a card from Charles. During the afternoon, Joan roused for a moment, pointed at the roses, and uttered one word: "Charles?" Frances said, "Yes." Joan smiled broadly at her mother and immediately drifted back to sleep. In the twilight of her dreams, Joan hoped that one day she would call him "Daddy."

Two Are Better Than One

Frances left the hospital that night with much on her mind. She had carried the load of being a single parent for most of her children's lives. All she could think was, *Oh, Charles, I wish you were here.*

Upon arriving home, she called him immediately and shared the day's events. She mentioned that Joan had uttered only one word all day—his name. The following day, Charles sent Joan a telegram, specially delivered to her hospital room.

Charles' favorite picture of Frances, which she sent to him before they were married.

Charles had not mentioned marriage to Frances, but he was beginning to write about solving problems together. His thoughts were often on such details as transporting books and keeping records as she traveled. He even projected that the books she had already written were just the beginning of many more that she would eventually author. His thoughts were constantly on how he could help her.

Tom Steder met Charles for the first time over the phone. Tom later asked his mother to describe Mr. Hunter. Frances responded, "Well, he has a beautiful soul, and our relationship is Christ-centered, and that's all that matters."

Tom responded, "Do you think that is enough?"

Frances answered with complete honesty, "Is there anything else?"

Shortly after her conversation with Tom, Frances was on a flight that, once she and other passengers had disembarked, would continue on to Houston. Like a teenage girl with a crush, she sent Charles a note via the flight attendant, to be mailed in Houston.

Nothing Is Impossible!

One weekend when Frances left home, she was hoping that the weekend of ministry in this particular church would totally occupy her mind, thus taking her thoughts off of Charles. What she experienced was the "deadest" church she had ever seen. The more positively she preached, the more negatively the people responded. They could not understand how Frances could have an exciting relationship with God. They did not expect anyone in their church to get saved and didn't know what to do with them if they did. Frances ministered Friday and Saturday with no visible results, and she became totally frustrated and completely exhausted.

On Sunday morning, she ended her message by trying one last time to get the attention of the congregation. With all the lung power she had left, she screamed at the crowd, "Nothing is impossible with God! Nothing is impossible with God! Nothing, nothing, nothing!"

The third time she said this, Frances suddenly realized that she was standing before the people and telling them that nothing was impossible with God, when she had been telling God that in her own life, love and marriage were impossibilities.

Frances gave the shortest altar call of her career. "If you've got a problem, bring it to the altar, and God will answer it!"

Frances suddenly realized that she was standing before the people and telling them that nothing was impossible with God, when she had been telling God that in her own life, love and marriage were impossibilities.

Frances was the first person at the altar. She laid Charles Hunter on that altar. She quietly prayed, "God, let me know what to do with him; if he has no place in my life, get him out of my mind, my thoughts, and my heart!" Peace immediately flooded her soul. She wasn't sure what the answer was, but she felt good about it.

Later that evening, she opened her Bible to Matthew 6:33: *"But strive first for the kingdom of God and his righteousness, and all these things will be given to you as well"* (NRSV). Her eyes then moved up to verse 25: *"Therefore I tell you, do not worry about your life..."* (NRSV). This was her answer! Because she had sought first the kingdom of God, God was adding Charles to her life. He was not sent from the devil to interfere with her ministry! God had sent him to be an asset to her and to the ministry to which God had called her. Frances wept with joy.

God had sent Charles to be an asset to Frances and to the ministry to which God had called her.

No Time for Two Years

Thanking the Lord for his marvelous blessings, she wrote a note to Charles that had just three words: "I LOVE YOU." She mailed the note from the airport when she was leaving to return home.

Charles was visiting his parents in Corpus Christi, and his mother said to him, "Are you going to marry this Frances? That is all you talk about."

He was utterly shocked at his mother's suggestion, but when he got back home, he sat down and wrote a letter to Frances in which he said, "I LOVE YOU." Frances later said that when the two airmail planes passed by each other, one delivering Charles' letter and one delivering Frances', they surely backed up in the air and kissed each other!

On December 7, Charles reached into his mailbox to pull out a handful of envelopes, leafing through them until he found one with Frances' familiar handwriting. He knew that she had been traveling and marveled that she had taken the time to send him a note from the airport, both on arriving and leaving.

As soon as he opened the envelope and read the three words in bold print, he called Frances. When she picked up her phone, she heard words that made her heart thump madly: "Honey, when can we be married?"

Charles didn't ask Frances, "Will you marry me?" but, "When?"

Frances replied, "Let me look at my date book!" Frances' appointment book controlled her life. She rifled through it frantically and found no dates open for the next two years.

She felt God would not be pleased if she placed her own desires above the calling on her life. Charles did not want the first thing he did as her husband to cause her to cancel a service. They both decided to pray and seek God in determining the date for their wedding.

On December 20, Frances' former mother-in-law, Mrs. Steder, died. As she prepared for the funeral of the woman who had been like a mother to her, she realized she wanted Charles in her life—not in two years, but now—to support her in ministry and give her the companionship she had not known she needed until his loving concern for her had penetrated her heart.

She cried out, "God, I just don't know when Charles and I can get married, but You do, so I am going to ask You to reveal to me and confirm to Charles exactly when we should be married."

Shortly after her prayer, the Lord spoke deeply within her spirit, "1969 was Jeanne's, 1970 is yours; start it off the very first minute of the year at the church's 'Party for the Lord' on New Year's Eve."

December 31 was only eleven days away. As soon as she could after the funeral, Frances called Charles, hoping he would be home, even though he normally would not be there so early in the day.

Yes or No—Will You Marry Me?

Charles had experienced an exhausting day, so he had decided to go home early. He walked in the door to hear the phone ringing. When he answered it, Frances blurted to him, "Charles, God has revealed to me exactly when we should be married. Now I want you to pray fervently and ask Him to confirm it to you." Charles agreed as Frances hung up before rushing to the service where she was to minister.

After Frances' call, Charles completed some errands and then returned home. He lay down to rest shortly after seven o'clock. At 8:20, the Lord awoke him with the answer that he was seeking.

At the end of the service, Frances went immediately to the pastor's house and called Charles. When he answered the phone, he said, "I wrote you a letter, and I want to read part of it to you." Frances thought it was ridiculous for him to read a letter that he was going to mail to her, but then she became excited because she would not have to wait!

Charles held the page in his strong, steady hands and, with emotion, read these words: "I feel utterly confident that your answer is the exact same date and exact time, and my heart is about to jump out of my chest." Frances' heart was pounding as she listened to him continue, "At the New Year's Eve party for the Lord, at midnight—to start the fabulous 1970 year." Charles then asked Frances, "By the way—will you marry me?"

Frances responded without hesitation by quoting the verses that the Lord had impressed upon her to memorize for the occasion when Charles would ask her to marry him:

> *Entreat me not to leave you, or to turn back from following after you; for wherever you go, I will go; and wherever you lodge, I will lodge; your people shall be my people, and your God, my God. Where you die, I will die, and there will I be buried. The Lord do so to me, and more also, if anything but death parts you and me.*
>
> (Ruth 1:16–17)

There was a pause as Frances waited breathlessly. Charles broke the silence with his quiet Texas drawl, asking, "Yes or no—will you marry me?"

Frances was taken aback. She thought that one of the most beautiful Scriptures in the Bible had profoundly expressed her acceptance. "Charles," she asked, "didn't you hear the Scriptures I just read?"

Charles spoke softly, "Yes, honey, I heard you say you'd run after me, and that you would live with me; but honey, I want you to marry me!"

Frances assured him that her answer was an unqualified "Yes!"

How Do I Know Thee?

Frances returned to Miami on December 22, and Charles was to arrive the next day. There were a few issues yet to be resolved. They were not sure they would recognize each other because of having seen each other for such a short time in Houston! Charles had told Frances that he wanted to see her wrapped up in a big bow with a tag that read, "Charles, I love you." Tom's wife had printed a Christmas tag saying, "For Charles, from God." Frances turned the card over and wrote, "I love you!"

Frances was also concerned about how she should greet Charles when she met him in the airport. They had never had an actual date, so she felt uncomfortable kissing him. She thought about shaking his hand, but that seemed rather formal for a man she was going to marry in a few days. On her way out the door, she saw a small poster taped above the light switch that said, "Lord, what wilt thou have me to do?" She ripped it off the wall and pinned it to her clothes. She went to the airport to meet her future husband with a Christmas bow in her hair, a big Christmas tag, and a sign saying, "Lord, what wilt thou have me to do?"

Frances was late arriving at the airport. She looked frantically for Charles all over the airport and even had him paged. Just as his name was announced over the loudspeaker, she turned around to see his tall frame and beaming smile. They spotted each other at the same instant.

Frances may have wondered what to do, but Charles had no such hesitation. He went right to her, took her in his arms, and kissed her tenderly. Frances wondered why she had ever brought that silly poster with her, because she knew this was exactly what the Lord would have them do!

Not a Minute to Spare

New Year's Eve was upon them, and Charles and Frances did not have their marriage license yet. Because Christmas had fallen just before the weekend, it was Monday, December 29, before they could apply for their license, and they were told that Charles could pick it up on December 31. However, when Charles went to pick up the license on Wednesday morning, the county clerk told him it would not be available until the morning of January 2.

"That's too late!" Charles exclaimed to the clerk. "God told us to be

Charles and Frances cutting their wedding cake on January 1, 1970.

married at a party for the Lord exactly one minute after the New Year."

"Who told you?" the clerk asked.

"God told us," Charles replied.

The clerk did not seem very sympathetic, but he allowed Charles to speak with the chief clerk, who gave him a slip of paper that would permit him to pick up the license at nine o'clock on January 1. That was still too late! Charles silently bombarded heaven with prayer and asked if he could go in to see the judge. The chief clerk went into the judge's chambers on Charles' behalf and came back out with the same slip of paper. This time, however, a line had been drawn through 9:00 a.m.; it now read 12:01 a.m., January 1, 1970.

The clerk said, "Take this to the judge's home tonight at exactly 12:01—not one minute before! He will give you your license. Here's the address."

On the evening of December 31, a policeman who was also a church member drove to the judge's home and picked up the license. After the praise celebration, Frances slipped into the back of the church and changed into her wedding dress.

At exactly midnight, Pastor Slagle asked the wedding party to step forward. Frances stood up, turned to fix her eyes on Charles, and approached him as though she were floating. Tears filled Charles' eyes as he watched his bride moving toward him. As bride and groom clasped hands to begin the rest of their life together, the policeman arrived with their marriage certificate and slipped it silently into the pastor's hand.

Chapter Seven

The Happy Hunters

Prior to their wedding, Charles had asked Frances if she would like to honeymoon in the Bahamas. She had to tell him that it wouldn't be possible to go on a honeymoon because she had a speaking engagement at a Christian college scheduled for January 2. Right before the wedding, however, she learned that she had made a mistake and the college would not even be open that day. Frances seldom made scheduling mistakes, so they agreed that God must have blocked out that day for them to have together.

God had orchestrated other things for them, as well. Long before Frances and Charles met, they both had decided to downsize their responsibilities. In Frances' case, it was her large home. It had been a wonderful house in which to raise her two children with its eight rooms, three bathrooms, and a swimming pool. It had even served as a halfway house for several years for young people who had accepted Christ and needed strong Christian nurturing for a while.

As Frances traveled more, often with Joan accompanying her, the house was more of a burden than a blessing. Even though there were emotional attachments, Frances felt the leading of God to sell it. She listed it with a realtor before she left for a lengthy tour in California. As she listed it, she prayed, "Lord, if You want me to sell this house, sell it while I'm in California, so I won't be hurt if someone says, 'I don't like this' or, 'I don't like that.'"

The second day she was in California, she received a call with an offer on the house. Two days later, she had received two offers for the house, both for the full asking price. Frances signed all the papers for the sale while she was in California. When she returned home, she and Joan had just sixteen days to move, but they had nowhere to go. Frances prayed, and the Lord directed her to an apartment in a brand-new building, which was completed and ready for occupancy on the day she needed to be out of her house.

Charles had downsized his life in a different way. In the months before his first wife died, he had reduced his involvement in his CPA practice by 50 percent. After her death, he did not resume his former workload but instead dedicated more of his time to involvement with ministries through his church. Once he met Frances, he realized that God had been shifting his responsibilities so that he could be more focused on doing the Lord's work.

What's In a Name?

Charles asked Joan if he could adopt her so that she would be his very own daughter.

Immediately after they were married, Frances relocated to Houston. Joan remained in Florida with Tom and his family to finish her junior year of high school. However, before leaving Florida, Charles had asked Joan if he could adopt her so that she would be his very own daughter. She was quick to respond, "Yes, yes, yes!"

Charles said that whenever Joan joined them in Houston, he wanted her to never experience being introduced first as Joan Gardner and then later as Joan Hunter. Before the end of January, they flew Joan to Houston. Joan arrived at night, and first thing the next morning, Charles and Frances took Joan to the courthouse and had her name changed to Hunter. Then, Joan flew back to Florida.

By Texas law, Charles and Frances had to be married for at least six months before Charles could adopt Joan. By the time Joan was out of school and able to move to Houston, the required six months had elapsed. The court sent someone to the Hunters' home to approve Charles as a father, and the two got so involved talking about the Lord that the caseworker forgot to get all of the information she needed, so the process was delayed.

On September 14, 1970, Charles proudly took Joan to court to complete the adoption. The State of Texas granted her a brand-new birth certificate, showing that she belonged to Charles and Frances Hunter just as if she had been born to them. Since then, the family has teased Joan because each year she celebrates two birthdays but grows only one year older! Although they had to wait until September for the adoption to be final, Charles received the desire of his heart, because from the month of January 1970, whenever Joan was introduced to anyone in Houston, it was as "Joan Hunter."

Frances' name was another matter. She had three best-selling books in print and many previously scheduled speaking engagements under the name "Frances Gardner." They agreed that she would keep her professional name for her ministry events; in their private lives, she would be Mrs. Charles Hunter.

Frances told Charles, "Honey, you are going to face many problems with this arrangement. Your ego is bound to bother you when I am introduced as Frances Gardner and you are not recognized as my husband."

Charles was certain that he was fully yielded to God and that "self" was dead.

When they had been married about six weeks and Frances was ministering out of town, Charles received a letter from her filled with newspaper clippings, bulletins, and other printed materials related to her trip. One clipping was a front-page article with a picture of Frances. Underneath, the caption read, "Frances Gardner speaks."

The clippings hit Charles like a bolt of lightning. It was difficult enough being away from his wife—when she was gone, he felt as though a part of his own arm had been ripped from him—but to see her former name glaring from all the news reports truly sent him to his knees to get victory over the flesh!

Later that evening, Frances called and said that the Lord had spoken to her. She realized she wanted nothing more than to be known as Mrs. Charles Hunter. She had already taken steps to change her bookings. For a while, she would be known as Frances Gardner Hunter, and then her name would naturally arrive at its perfect destination—Frances Hunter.

Occasionally, Charles and Joan would be able to fly to the city where Frances was ministering. On one such occasion, they arrived in California, and, over a period of several days, Frances was introduced as "Frances Hunter" and her husband was introduced as "Charles Gardner." Charles' ego certainly had an opportunity to resist pride! When the mistake was corrected, they were introduced as "Frances Hunter and her husband, Mr. Hunter."

A Servant's Heart

Before they were married, Charles had told Frances that it would be his honor just to carry her books. During the early months of their marriage, he did little else besides carrying all the cartons of books, unpacking them, arranging them on tables, and then counting and repacking them. Although he had been quite active in leadership roles in his church for many years and had served as the president of his CPA firm, he was content to serve her without acclaim.

Before they were married, Charles had told Frances that it would be his honor just to carry her books.

One of Charles' qualities that Frances appreciated deeply was that he was a true gentleman at all times. After their marriage, his gallantry did not fade. When they drove to their home in Houston and were about to enter the area that led to the garage, Frances, being a very independent woman, jumped out of the car and opened the big wooden doors. When Charles reached her, he had a look on his face that said, "Won't you let me be a gentleman?" Frances shut the doors, got back in the car, and allowed Charles to open them. She never opened the doors again.

Charles respected the calling of his wife and realized that she, like he, was tired after a trip or a day in the office. He made it a point to help with chores around the house. In the kitchen, Frances was the cook, but Charles cleaned up after her so that when they sat down to eat dinner, the kitchen was already clean. He not only treated his wife as a queen, but he also treated friends and guests as though they were royalty.

A Little Home Bible Study

In time, Frances was able to arrange her schedule so that she and Charles could begin a small, unadvertised Bible study in their home. The first week, there were six people in addition to Charles and Frances. The second week, the number more than doubled. Each week thereafter, the group grew until they had one hundred and twenty-three people in their home. Theirs was a nice, large home, but Frances recalls, "People were hanging from the chandeliers!"

When they moved the Bible study to a hotel, the room they used the first week was not large enough the second week. Each ensuing week, the hotel would move them to the next larger room. When they reached four hundred people, they moved the "little home Bible study" to a nearby high school auditorium.

As they began to pray for the sick, they trained their board members to help them minister to the growing crowd. During this time, God spoke to them with a word of prophecy that would come to pass more than thirty years later: "The day will come when you will stand in the Astrodome with one hundred and twenty healing teams ministering healing to the body of Christ."

Frances and Charles were amazed to watch their Bible study increase from six to over a thousand people in a few months. They were just beginning to see what God could do with a wild sinner and a dried-up spiritual prune who were totally consumed with joy and love for Him and had a vision to reach the world.

Frances and Charles' Bible study increased from six to over a thousand people in a few months.

Praise the Lord Anyway!

Charles had been tested in his spiritual humility when his brand-new wife was better known by another name and when, during their early ministry trips, he was either known as her book table assistant or was overlooked entirely. Frances was soon to experience her own test of humility.

In July 1970, Frances was selected to be the pacesetting speaker for the International Christian Booksellers Convention. It was a tremendous honor to speak to an assembly of people responsible for getting books into the hands of the reading public. Even though she had written three best-selling books in two years, Frances was a relatively new author, so she was excited beyond words.

She bought a new outfit for the occasion and could hardly sleep the night before, tossing and turning with anticipation. The next day, when it was her turn to speak, she prayed and ministered with the joy and enthusiasm for which she was becoming well-known.

When she finished, several people from the crowd came onto the stage to congratulate her and shake her hand. All of a sudden, the platform began to wobble. The unsteady construction was made of several folding tables that had been pushed together, and the table on which Frances was standing on began to collapse. Charles was standing next to her on another table but could not reach her.

To Frances, it seemed that she was in a slow-motion movie; she realized she was going down but knew she could do absolutely nothing to stop the inevitable. Both the table and Frances crashed to the floor with a heart-stopping thud. Her glasses fell off, her wig fell off, and she was sprawled on the floor in the most undignified of positions in her new dress. She grabbed her wig and put it on sideways, while her natural hair hung in strands down the middle of her face. She had sustained no physical injuries, however, and she immediately demonstrated the joyful disposition that multitudes would come to love. In her most impressive public appearance to date, while still lying on the floor, she loudly proclaimed, "Praise the Lord anyway!"

The audience cheered with appreciation as they realized that Frances lived the life of praise that she talked about.

A Moment to Treasure

Frances has a very poignant memory that involves Charles' father. Shortly after she and Charles were married, Charles took her to Corpus Christi to meet his parents. His father was terminally ill and lived in a nursing home. When the couple went into his room, he was lying in a comatose condition. Charles patted him and spoke gently, saying, "Papa, I want you to meet my bride. This is Frances. I've told her about you and Mama and all of us kids."

Charles continued to coax his father for a few minutes. As he and Frances stood holding hands by the bedside, his dad's eyes opened momentarily, and he said, "Once I was a sinner..." before lapsing back into the coma.

A few minutes later, he came out of the coma again and said, "...but then I got saved." He closed his eyes again. Charles and Frances leaned over, kissed him gently, and prayed. Just a few days later, he went to be with the Lord, who had wonderfully saved him. The words he said to his son and new daughter-in-law were his last.

Charles' Humble Spirit

Charles was always protective of his wife. Whenever Frances went up onstage to speak, Charles would escort her, gently holding her arm as she walked to her position at the podium. He would make sure she had the microphone, then would lovingly pat her on the back and turn to stand inconspicuously behind her. Frances felt secure knowing he was always standing nearby, occasionally patting her on the back and giving her his total and complete approval.

Whenever Frances went up onstage to speak, Charles would escort her, gently holding her arm as she walked to her position at the podium.

He remained in the background until, one night, the anointing of God was evident upon him, and the two became cospeakers from that time onward. Both ministered in their unique gifts and also flowed together as one.

In the beginning, Charles would always pay his own travel expenses for any trips on which he was able to accompany his wife. By the end of 1970, the Hunters had invested five thousand dollars of their own money to cover travel expenses. Within a year, God had covered not only all their ministry expenses, but also enough extra money to repay them the five thousand dollars.

Charles longed to be with Frances on each and every ministry engagement, and he cut back his involvement with his CPA firm as much as possible. He had worked with his three older partners for more than twenty years when, just after he and Frances were married, four younger men joined the firm. With Charles often away, the seven partners began to clash. The older men were set in their ways and reluctant to listen to the younger partners' new ideas, while the young men were frustrated at the others' unwillingness to change. Charles tried to mediate the situation, but he knew it would not be resolved.

He and the younger men stepped away from the original firm and began a new partnership. Charles brought experience and credibility to the firm, along with many established clients. The young men brought enthusiasm and willingness to work the many hours necessary to build a business.

At the time, Charles and Frances were not receiving a salary from the ministry. Both realized that starting a new business would affect their income, but they knew God would supply all their needs. With the firm in good hands, Charles continued to cut back his involvement until, by February 1973, he was working nearly full-time in ministry with Frances. In September 1975, as they were walking hand-in-hand through O'Hare Airport, the Lord spoke to Charles. He turned to Frances and said, "God just told me to retire from my accounting practice."

Frances enthusiastically responded, "That's exactly what He just said to me!" As soon as they returned to Houston, Charles began making arrangements to turn over the CPA firm completely to his partners. By the end of the month, the Happy Hunters were in full-time ministry together.

THE GROWING MINISTRY

When Charles and Frances were married, Frances moved into the house Charles had inhabited with his late wife. It was a spacious home with a nice office area that Charles used whenever he brought work home with him. Next to his office was a large walk-in closet that provided more than enough room for Frances to convert this space into an office of her own. For the next few years of their ministry, she answered correspondence sent by churches around the nation from her closet office, where she also produced and mailed monthly newsletters that helped build a support base for the ministry.

As the ministry grew, the office space, as well as Frances' time, became inadequate to handle all the office work required. They hired a secretary who came to work in their house. But in just a few months, they needed to lease office space outside of their home for the first time in their ministry. The ministry outgrew that space in a short time, too, so they next purchased land to build their own ministry offices.

The day they moved into their first building, they felt like it was so big that they would never be able to fill it up. Yet, just as with the tiny Bible study that had outgrown their home and then the church, they outgrew this facility faster than they could comprehend.

God Intervenes for a New Building

Their first building was still brand-new when they began to wonder how they were going to function in a facility they had outgrown so quickly. One afternoon, a woman came by to give them a check for $150. She said, "God told me to give this to you for your new building."

Frances said to her, "You've got to be kidding! We're not going to build another building."

Her response was, "But God said you were."

Charles and Frances always tried to be sensitive to the Spirit of God, so they did not dismiss the woman's words. But their building was on a corner lot. The only expansion that could take place would have to be to the north, and that was a property much too large for them to consider purchasing.

The next morning, the telephone rang. It was the businessman who owned the property just north of theirs, and he was calling to tell them that somebody wanted to purchase two-thirds of the property but did not want the remaining one-third, which was right next to them. He was wondering if they would be interested in it.

Charles asked the man how much he wanted for the property. He replied, "a dollar and thirty-five cents per square foot, which comes to about forty thousand dollars."

Charles said to him, "Just a moment, please!" He looked upward and said, "God, shall we buy it?" A second elapsed, and Charles responded to the businessman, "Yes!"

"When do you want to close?" asked the man.

"Just a moment, please," Charles replied. He prayed again, "God, when do we want to close?" Charles then spoke into the telephone, "As soon as possible!"

"How do you want to pay for it? By cash, a loan with your bank, or a loan with us?"

"Just a moment, please." Charles prayed and then answered, "Cash!"

"How about a week from Wednesday? Is that all right?" asked the man.

One last time, Charles responded, "Just a moment, please." Again, he sought God's answer and replied, "Wednesday is fine!"

Charles hung up the phone and looked at Frances. They both knew the reality. The ministry had never been as low on funds as it was at that moment. The Hunters' personal account was inadequate, as well. But they were certain of one thing: the Lord had spoken to them. They had to obey!

They went to church on Sunday and gave one hundred dollars as a regular tithe and then wrote a check for an additional four hundred dollars as seed faith for the forty thousand dollars they would need. They were putting their trust in two verses from Scripture:

> *And anyone who gives up his home, brothers, sisters, father, mother, wife, children, or property, to follow me, shall receive a hundred times as much in return, and shall have eternal life.*
>
> (Matthew 19:29 TLB)

> *For if you give, you will get! Your gift will return to you in full and overflowing measure, pressed down, shaken together to make room for more, and running over. Whatever measure you use to give—large or small—will be used to measure what is given back to you.*
> (Luke 6:38 TLB)

They had a service on Monday and didn't get back to the office until Tuesday evening. Just before the property closing to be held on Wednesday, there was exactly forty thousand dollars in the Hunter Ministries bank account. It was the largest amount of money ever to come into the ministry within forty-eight hours up to that point! They had acted in complete obedience to the direction of the Lord. God had honored their faith as they knew He would.

They acted in complete obedience to the direction of the Lord, and God honored their faith as they knew He would.

Chapter Eight

Partnering with the Holy Spirit

From the instant that Frances asked Jesus into her heart, she had saturated herself in the Word of God. The more she read, the more she realized how limited most believers are in their concepts of God. No matter which translation she used, every one of her Bibles depicted a God who was mighty, a God who passionately loved His children, a God who came to the rescue of those who called on Him—a God who wanted His earthly family healthy, prosperous, and victorious over every adversary.

> *The more Frances read the Word of God, the more she realized how limited most believers are in their concepts of God.*

When Charles surrendered all of himself to the Lord and began to search the Bible with all of his heart and soul, he realized there was much more to his loving heavenly Father than he had ever heard about in church. He began to yearn to see God manifest His will today as He had in Bible times. When he and Frances were married, they searched the Word of God together and agreed that wherever they went, they would pray for the sick and believe in God's power to heal them.

In their meetings, once in a great while, someone would be healed, but most of the time nothing happened. The more they searched the Scriptures, however, the more convinced they became that healing was God's will, and they asked Him to show them the key to helping people receive healing.

God, I Want All of You Except...

Frances always encouraged people to get everything from God that they could. A few of her friends took her advice to heart and asked God to baptize them with the Holy Spirit. When they excitedly told Frances that they could speak in tongues, she expressed her joy for them but conveyed that she and Charles really didn't need the baptism.

Many times, people approached Frances to ask her, with a superior and condemning attitude, "Have you received the baptism with the Holy Spirit?"

Frances would reply diplomatically, "Oh, yes! God has baptized me with His Holy Spirit, but it isn't necessary to speak in tongues, if that's what you mean."

The offended person would walk away, and Frances began to draw back from "super Christians" who, according to 1 Corinthians 13:1, were just making noise. On her travels, enlightened people often stuck copies of John and Elizabeth Sherrill's book, *They Speak with Other Tongues*, into Frances' purse or suitcase. As soon as Frances got to the airport, she would toss all the books into the nearest trash can. Charles commented once that she would really be surprised when one of those trash cans began speaking in tongues as she passed by!

Frances responded to the love of God as positively as she rejected the condemnation of others.

A friend who wrote Frances a letter in genuine love finally got her attention as she shared what the Lord had done for her through the baptism with the Holy Spirit. Frances responded to the love of God as positively as she had rejected the condemnation of others. Her interest was piqued enough that she began reading books on the subject.

One of the books that made an outstanding impression on the Hunters was Pat Boone's new release, *A New Song*. Their spirits leapt as they saw in this book an emphasis on the Giver and not the gift. The baptism was described as an added dimension to life that would enable a child of God to better worship and serve Him. That was exactly what they wanted to do! They wrote an enthusiastic letter to the Boones telling them how the book had affected their lives. In it, they said,

> Pat and Shirley, your book was like a light from heaven. We have constantly cautioned people not to be legalistic but to give God the freedom to work in and through them. Your book showed us what we have been doing. We have been saying to God, "We want everything You have got—except tongues!" How foolish it is to limit God this way. If you want all that God has, you can't limit Him!

A few months later, Charles and Frances were in Pittsburgh and found themselves with a free evening. It was the first time in their ministry that this had ever happened. They looked in the paper for a service that they could attend and spotted a charismatic conference being held at a Presbyterian church. Frances had been invited to speak at a charismatic gathering in Miami later that month, so they decided it would be a good idea to attend a charismatic service and see what it was all about. They were very apprehensive, but God nudged them in their spirits to be there.

Usually, when they were in a meeting of Christians, the Hunters sat as close to the front as possible, because they wanted to be where the action was. However, when they arrived at the Presbyterian church, they were very careful to sit near an exit so that they could make a quick escape if there were any problems. They had heard stories from their non-Pentecostal friends about churches that would invite people to be filled with the Spirit and then take them to the basement and beat them on the head until, at last, moaning and groaning, the people would say, "I've got it!" just to make the beating stop. Charles and Frances wanted to be near a door they could escape before anyone began pounding on their heads!

The evening began with a worship service that included many familiar songs, but they seemed different, as if the praise were alive with joy and power. At one point, as if on cue, the voices suddenly shifted to a perfectly harmonized chorus that the Hunters could not understand. The sound rose to a beautiful spine-tingling crescendo, and then, again as if on cue, it stopped. Except for an occasional "Alleluia," Charles and Frances did not understand one word, but it was the most beautiful singing they had ever heard.

The worship leader seemed to glow with the love of God. He invited the congregants to stand, form little cups with their hands, and lift them unto the Lord as they sang a beautiful hymn of dedication, "Fill My Cup, Lord." Often, because of her enthusiasm and desire to participate in worship,

Frances had raised one hand to show her agreement with a stirring song, but to lift both hands was unthinkable! She and Charles bent down behind the pews so no one would see them, but before the song ended, they were on their feet, their cups lifted up to receive all they could of God.

Just as Charles and Frances were feeling totally comfortable in the charismatic service, the speaker invited anyone who wanted to be baptized in the Holy Spirit to stand and go through a side door and down to the basement, where designated people would pray with them. Charles and Frances glanced at each other. They were not about to go any place for someone to beat on them, so they made a quick exit and ran all the way to their car!

A Long, Skinny Finger Beckoned

Charles and Frances had heard of the healing evangelist Kathryn Kuhlman, but they had never attended one of her services. Miss Kuhlman was to speak at the First Presbyterian Church of Pittsburgh the next morning, and a friend offered to take them to the service.

They arrived early, but the crowd waiting outside was already so large that they were certain they would not get a seat. They noticed a little girl whose skin was covered with big lumps and who appeared to be close to death. They stepped back to allow her family to move ahead of them. Suddenly, an usher appeared and asked, "Would Charles and Frances Hunter step this way, please?"

Somehow, Miss Kuhlman had learned that a famous author was outside. Frances did not think that her little paperback books, which sold for seventy-five cents each, qualifed her to be a famous author, but in obedience, she and Charles followed the usher inside and down the aisle to a seat on the second row. Soon after they were seated, the service began with stirring worship. Then, Miss Kuhlman came from behind the curtain and joined the huge choir in singing "How Great Thou Art." She taught a short message and then looked out into the audience. There was expectancy in the air.

As Charles and Frances sat, spellbound, their hearts beat as one with the anticipation of seeing what a mighty God was going to do before their eyes. People came forward testifying that God had healed them as they were sitting in the crowd. Some came down from the top rows of the balcony and said that God had touched them way up there.

At each report, Miss Kuhlman would lift a flowing gossamer-sleeved arm to heaven and break out in joyous thanksgiving for what God had done. Then, to the Hunters' amazement, she would gently touch the people, and they would fall backward to the floor! A group of twenty-five nuns came forward, and when Miss Kuhlman touched one of them, the other twenty-four fell down like bowling pins. The Hunters were sitting close enough to see that Miss Kuhlman had a small, fragile frame, and it would not be possible for her to push over one person, much less entire groups at one time, with her own strength.

Frances was amazed that Miss Kuhlman seemed to know things without being told about them. Standing before the audience, she pointed to a certain section of the church and said, "A man over there has just been healed of a leg problem. He is wearing a brace on his left leg. Take off the brace and come here."

Miss Kuhlman seemed to know things without being told about them.

The man stood, took a brace off of his left leg, and walked to her with no difficulty whatsoever. Then, Miss Kuhlman reached out to touch him, and he crumpled to the floor.

Miss Kuhlman then said to the congregation, "There is a little girl right back there who had cancer with big lumps all over her body. God just healed you, honey. Come here!"

The little girl whom Charles and Frances had seen outside the building ran down the aisle, healthy and robust, without a blemish on her body.

Frances had never seen anyone operate in a "word of knowledge." She and Charles could not explain what they were seeing, but they knew it was all wonderfully supernatural.

After she blessed the little girl, Miss Kuhlman looked toward heaven and waved her arm, her filmy sleeve rippling as she said, "Thanks a million, Jesus!" Her face radiated with love for the Lord.

Then, Miss Kuhlman paused. Frances and Charles waited breathlessly for what was next. She said to the congregation, "The power of the Spirit of God is present. I am no longer needed on this stage, and I am going to walk down onto the floor and move into the aisles. I don't want anyone to speak. I don't want anyone to reach out to me unless I request it. We must honor the presence of God. We must have reverence for the precious Holy Spirit."

Miss Kuhlman walked back and forth across the large auditorium. She moved up and down several aisles. The power of the Holy Spirit hovered over the crowd like a cloud. The silence was almost deafening, and the building seemed charged with electricity.

The first person she motioned to was Ralph Wilkerson, pastor of Melodyland Church in Anaheim, California. She laid her hands on him and said, "Jesus, bless him," and he dropped like a rock. The ushers helped him to stand up again. Again, she laid her hands on him, and again he went down. As he lay there, he did not appear to have been hurt by his fall. In fact, he looked very peaceful, like he was in the presence of God.

Miss Kuhlman looked around the congregation again. Frances had a funny feeling inside, and she braced herself. She would have made herself smaller if she could. But she could not hide. Suddenly, Miss Kuhlman looked straight at Frances and motioned with her long, slender finger for her to step out into the aisle. Frances was unsure what to do. She was wearing her best dress because she was scheduled to speak later that afternoon. However, she had made up her mind to experience all that God had in store for her. If this was of God, she did not want to miss it. She stood up and stepped out into the aisle.

As Frances basked in God's presence, she knew that her life would never be the same!

Miss Kuhlman placed her hands ever so gently on Frances' temples and said, "Jesus, bless my sister!" The next thing Frances knew, she was lying flat on the floor. She felt as though the Spirit of God had breathed on her and she had floated into heaven. It intrigued her that, as a large person, she had felt as light as a feather as she went to the floor. As she basked in God's presence, she knew that her life would never be the same!

Charles Gets the Rebound

Charles and Frances followed Kathryn Kuhlman's ministry for the rest of her life. They attended her services whenever possible and often were invited to participate, either as ushers or in other capacities. They were hungry for the power of God and willing to do whatever they were asked.

In a Houston service, Charles stood onstage beside Miss Kuhlman and watched as people fell, one after another, as the power of God flowed into them through her. Occasionally, someone seemed to resist the flow of God's power. At those times, Miss Kuhlman would step aside so that the power surge from God would not cause her to fall as it bounced off the resistant person. When she stepped aside, Charles stepped up, received the power, and fell to the floor. He was slain in the Spirit several times that afternoon. The catchers would help him up, and he would wait for the next rebound.

On one occasion, Charles and Frances discovered they were flying on the same plane as Miss Kuhlman. They landed in Chicago's O'Hare Airport and had a short layover before the Hunters flew on to Houston and Miss Kuhlman to Pittsburgh. Charles asked the ladies if they would like ice cream cones. Charles handed one to Miss Kuhlman, and then they each had to hurry to board their flights. It was a memorable day for Charles and Frances because the last time they ever saw Kathryn Kuhlman, she was licking that ice cream cone. She died just a few months later.

Kathryn Kuhlman's life, her relationship with Jesus, and the profound anointing upon her ministry impacted Charles and Frances significantly. In times to come, they felt that a portion of her anointing had been transferred to them.

In times to come, Charles and Frances felt that a portion of Kathryn Kuhlman's anointing had been transferred to them.

The Miami Charismatic Conference

Frances placed a call to her former pastor before leaving for the Miami Charismatic Conference. "Pastor Slagle," she said, "please round up everybody in the church that you know will pray for me this week. I'm supposed to minister in a charismatic conference in Miami, and I need all of you to pray that God will protect me from anything all those 'tongues people' might try to do to me.

"Charles and I went to a conference like this in Pittsburgh, and when they asked for people to come forward to receive the baptism with the Holy Spirit, they told them they would all go to the basement to be prayed for. If something is from God, I can't imagine why they wouldn't want everybody to witness it. That's when Charles and I left and ran all the way to the car! So you be sure to pray, pray, pray!"

Several of Frances' church friends accompanied her to the Miami conference. It opened with a worship service that seemed to draw the presence of God into the auditorium. It ended with the huge gathering singing "in the Spirit," after which there was a moment of holy silence. Frances tried to ignore the goose bumps that covered her during the worship.

A hush fell over the congregation. Frances felt that the Spirit of the Lord was so powerfully present that she could almost reach out and touch Him. She ministered in a strong anointing and closed with prayer. As she stood before the congregation, God gave her a specific instruction. In a spirit of reverence, she asked everyone to take a moment and reflect upon their lives. There was a holy silence. Then, someone began to speak in a lovely and soothing flow of words that she did not understand. When the words ended, another voice from another section of the room spoke in English, "The words you have heard from the lips of Frances Hunter are not her words. They are Mine. Take heed and obey."

Frances felt the room pulsing with the love of God in a way she could not describe. She wondered silently if there was something she was missing that God had for her.

As Frances' friends drove her to the airport after the conference, each one could still feel the presence of the Lord upon them. Finally, one of them said, "You know, if I had to make a choice between being dried-up or emotional, I'd pick being emotional. How about you?"

Frances had no choice but to answer the question honestly, "So would I."

Charles' Spiritual Journey

When Charles' family got saved, they knew the Lord had affected their lives dramatically, but they were careful to warn the children to stay away from "tongue talkers." Even though Charles had been cautioned about "false emotionalism and gibberish," he visited a Pentecostal tent meeting when he was fourteen. There, he saw a young girl who had humbly gone forward to receive the Holy Spirit being coached in what turned out to be nothing more than a performance for the altar worker's own ego. He was totally turned off by the experience.

In 1968, when he unreservedly surrendered his life to the Lord, Charles began to study God's Word with an open mind. He practically lived in the New Testament for a year following that commitment and knew that he had much spiritual growth ahead for him if he was serious about giving God complete control of his life.

God brought a deeply spiritual man into Charles' life—a man in whom Charles had great confidence. This man discussed the concepts of baptism with the Holy Spirit and speaking in tongues as he shared his personal experience, and one thing he said surprised Charles. He explained that he could speak in tongues anytime he wanted. Until then, Charles had thought speaking in tongues was something that would come unexpectedly and would do uncontrollable things to a person. Having someone he highly respected witness to him gave Charles a willingness to do anything the Lord asked of him, including speaking in tongues.

Having someone he highly respected witness to him gave Charles a willingness to do anything the Lord asked of him, including speaking in tongues.

Pursuing the Adventure

In the summer of 1971, Charles and Frances were in Denver at the International Christian Booksellers Convention. While autographing books at their booth, they noticed a sign identifying a booth nearby for George Otis. George had written a best-selling book entitled *You Shall Receive,* which was a chronicle of his exciting spiritual journey. He had been quoted frequently in Pat and Shirley Boone's book, so the Hunters were thrilled to have the opportunity to meet him.

George had been interested in the Hunters' ministry ever since they spoke in Hawaii, and he greeted them enthusiastically. He mentioned that Pat and Shirley were also at the conference, and they all met together later that afternoon for a time of prayer. As the five shared the exhilarating things God was doing in their lives, Charles and Frances strained to listen to every word anyone said about the Holy Spirit. An unexplainable excitement was building inside of them.

As the convention drew to a close, Frances could not get away from the gnawing feeling that she and Charles needed to spend some time with George. Since they traveled so much, they rarely invited anyone into their home, but before George left, they mentioned that he was welcome to stay in their guest room if he was ever in the Houston area. It was a noncommittal suggestion, and they felt certain he would never accept the invitation.

In August, Frances underwent eye surgery again. The day she got home from the hospital, she received a call from George Otis' secretary. George was scheduled to minister in Houston and wanted to take them up on their offer to stay in their guest room. He would be there on Saturday night, if that would be acceptable. Frances felt that she had no choice but to open their home to him, even though it was not the most convenient time to do so.

After she hung up the phone, Frances could not believe that she had just agreed to have a guest so soon after her surgery. She called Charles, hoping that he would respond in his usual protective manner, "I know you must still be weak, honey. Let me call their office and tell them Mr. Otis will have to stay somewhere else."

Instead, Charles said, "Honey, that's great! And don't worry; God will give you all the strength you need."

Since it was apparent that George was going to be their guest, Frances decided it would be rude to host a noted author without first reading his book. She had to hunt for the book for a while; they had hidden it for fear guests who came to the house might think they were interested in "tongues." She read a few pages before she nodded off to sleep, exhausted from her stay in the hospital. When she awoke, she picked up the book again and couldn't put it down until she had completed it. As she closed the book, something inside her knew what was about to happen in her and Charles' lives.

Charles and Frances were to pick up George after he spoke at a Full Gospel Businessmen's meeting on Saturday morning. However, they felt it would be discourteous if they did not attend and listen to his testimony, so they went early and were seated as close to the podium as possible. They listened intently as George shared his adventure with God. When he invited those who wanted the baptism of the Holy Spirit to join him after the meeting, they tried to stand far enough away to not get involved but close enough to eavesdrop. However, friends kept coming up to them to talk, so they were unable to hear what he said.

When George invited those who wanted the baptism of the Holy Spirit to join him after the meeting, Charles and Frances tried to stand far enough away to not get involved but close enough to eavesdrop.

Afterward, they took George out for a quick lunch and learned that one of his Texas friends had invited him to stay with him while he was in Houston. George's friend wondered why he was staying with the Hunters. George's only explanation was that God had intervened in the phone wires to arrange his stay at their home.

That evening, George spoke at the University of Houston. Again, Charles and Frances tried to listen when he gave instructions regarding the indwelling of the Holy Spirit. Immediately, people gathered around them like long-lost friends, so again they could not hear what George was saying.

Do You Really Want It?

The next morning, Charles and Frances fixed breakfast for George before going to the church where he was to minister. Frances was about to burst. She and Charles had been with George all day and all night on Saturday, and they still had not talked with him about the Holy Spirit. They had not even heard anything when they tried to eavesdrop.

Finally, Frances said, "George, you know we don't speak in tongues, don't you?"

George responded, "No, I hadn't noticed," and resumed eating. He had purposely avoided bringing up the subject because he did not want to dampen the wonderful friendship that was developing with the Hunters.

Frances felt compelled to explain, "We believe there is a genuine gift of tongues. There was a time when we told God we didn't want it, but we've realized how wrong that was. So we've told God that if He wants to, He can give it to us. But we're not going to go out of our way to get it, because we just don't think we need it."[5]

George's response was in perfect love, but it hit Frances at the core of her being: "I know the power you've got in your life because I've seen the evidence of what happened while you were in Hawaii. But wouldn't you like to have more power from God?"

"Frances, you've already got one hotline to heaven. Wouldn't you like to have two—one in English and one in a heavenly language?"

He went on, using an analogy from Frances' book *Hot Line to Heaven.* "Frances, you've already got one hotline to heaven. Wouldn't you like to have two—one in English and one in a heavenly language?"

Frances replied, "Well, then, let Him give it to me."

"God doesn't work that way," George patiently explained. "He won't force the baptism on you any more than He will force salvation on anyone. You have to take the first step; then, God will do the rest."

As they finished their breakfast and got in the car to take George to the airport, Frances began to panic because she knew he would not be coming back to their house. She knew that God had sent him to speak more into their lives, but they were running out of time. She asked George if he had a tape or anything with teaching about the Holy Spirit. As the Lord would have it, George had one unedited tape in his suitcase. It was the only tape he had made up to that time, and he had felt compelled to finish it just before coming to Houston.

[5] Charles and Frances Hunter, *The Two Sides of a Coin* (Kingwood, TX: Hunter Books, 1973), 54.

We Want It!

It was late that evening when they got home, and Frances was exhausted. When she suggested they listen to the tape, Charles discerned that she really needed to rest and proposed that they wait until the next day.

On Monday, while Charles was at work, Frances reread all the passages in the Scriptures about speaking in tongues. For the first time, she saw that the disciples would recognize others as being filled with the Holy Spirit when they heard them speaking in tongues. She saw that there were two kinds of tongues—one for your daily prayer life and one for public ministry, as one of the nine gifts of the Holy Spirit. Gradually, all of her hang-ups vanished, and she could not wait until she and Charles would listen to George's tape.

Once Charles was home, they gulped down their supper, finished their chores, and retired to the bedroom to listen to the tape. Charles placed the cassette in their tape player and pressed the play button. As they listened to George outline his glorious journey, they were mesmerized. When the tape ended, Charles turned it over and played it again. Then, they listened to it a third time.

Finally, they were hearing the instructions that had eluded them. George said, "Talk to Jesus. Ask Him to baptize you with the Holy Spirit. He is the Baptizer." The tape explained, "The Lord said that if you ask for bread, He will not give you a stone, if you ask for a fish, He won't give you a snake, and if you ask for an egg, He won't give you a scorpion. When you ask Him for the Holy Spirit, you will receive the Holy Spirit. Ask Him…and then speak as the Spirit gives you utterance."

"Talk to Jesus. Ask Him to baptize you with the Holy Spirit. He is the Baptizer."

Last, George suggested that they raise their hands in worship and surrender to God, and then "make some syllable sounds, not in English, and the Holy Spirit will take whatever sounds you make and turn them into a heavenly language."

Charles lifted his hands. Frances lifted her hands. They lay there side by side in their bed, hands raised in worship to God. But when the time came to speak, nothing came out of their mouths. They went through the process several times with no results and ended up only laughing hysterically. They decided that it might be better for each of them to be alone when asking God for baptism with the Holy Spirit.

I Got It!

The next day, Frances listened to the tape again. Before she prayed for the baptism, she recalled that God had made the water solid under Peter as he stepped out of the boat. She lifted her hands to heaven and pleaded with all of her heart and soul, "God, if it's genuine, if it's real, if it's You, and if it's for me, then make the water hard, or in my case, make the air solid under the sound of my voice, and Jesus, I ask You to baptize me with the Holy Spirit."

She opened her mouth, made a few sounds, and instantly began praying in other tongues. The entire bedroom seemed to glow with the love of God. She prayed in tongues as she laid on the bed with her hands in the air, enveloped in the presence of God. She had never felt closer to God, more loved by Him, more protected by Him, more sheltered by Him, or more filled with love and praise for Him than in those moments.

As soon as she was willing to pause from her euphoria, she called Charles on the phone to share with him what the Lord had done. "Honey, it's true! It's genuine, it's real, and I've got it!" she said, and she began to cry.

Then Charles began to cry, too. "Let me hear you," he said to her.

Frances thought that both hands had to be raised in the air for an individual to speak in tongues, and she told him she didn't think it was possible for her to do while holding the phone. Charles said again, "Please try, honey!" Frances scrunched down in the bed, cradled the phone against her shoulder, and put her hands in the air. Over the telephone, she prayed in her heavenly language as Charles listened.

When she had finished praying in tongues, she prayed in comprehensible English, "Lord, so that we will stay on the same spiritual level, I'm going to ask that You baptize Charles with the Holy Spirit and give him a heavenly language in the car on the way home tonight."

Charles was so thrilled for Frances and so eager to get into his car and drive home that the day seemed like it would never end. At five o'clock, he straightened up his desk, locked the office door, and rushed to the car. He carefully made his way through the Houston traffic toward the freeway. God seemed to move cars out of the way as Charles drove around the first curve and onto the highway.

At last, he was able to pray, "Jesus, I ask You to baptize me with the Holy Spirit and give me a heavenly language, just as You gave Frances." Raising his hands to the Lord while driving sixty miles an hour was a challenge, so Charles kept his hands on the steering wheel. He opened his mouth and uttered one or two sounds, and the Lord took over from there. Out of his mouth poured a beautiful and fluent heavenly language. Charles' heart overflowed with the joy of the Lord. As he drove down the freeway, the love of God overpowered him, and he praised his Savior in the glory of the Holy Spirit.

When Frances was not traveling, Charles always anticipated her welcoming him at the door with loving hugs and kisses. That evening, Frances and Joan were not home when he arrived, but Charles didn't mind! He went into his office, lifted his hands as high as he could, and continued to pray in his beautiful new language. When Frances and Joan pulled into the driveway, Charles ran out to meet them. It was obvious from the expression on his face what had happened to him. He embraced Frances, nearly knocking her off her feet, and exclaimed, "I did!"

What Happened?

The impact on their personal lives was immediate. Charles said that the baptism with the Holy Spirit removed a veil that had dimmed his vision of Jesus. Frances said that the baptism gave her a greater ability to love God than she had ever dreamed possible. She had always accepted God's love for her, but she had never been able to return it in the way she had longed to.

Charles said that the baptism with the Holy Spirit removed a veil that had dimmed his vision of Jesus. Frances said that the baptism gave her a greater ability to love God than she had ever dreamed possible.

Both Charles and Frances immediately experienced a new zeal for reading and studying the Bible and a better spiritual understanding of the Scriptures. They were able to pray in the Spirit with confidence when they did not know how to pray for a situation in the natural. Their desire to see people move from defeated lives to abundant lives intensified. The baptism provided a new depth of guidance and understanding of God's will for their lives. And, if it were at all possible, they experienced even more joy!

You Can't Speak Here

Not long after they were baptized in the Holy Spirit, Frances was sitting at her desk and opening the morning mail when the phone rang. She answered in her usual way, "God is fabulous!"

A pastor she had known for several years identified himself to her and got right to the point. "I understand that George Otis spoke recently in a conference in Alaska, and he said you now speak in tongues. Is this information correct, Frances? Do you speak in tongues?"

Noting the chill in his voice, Frances chose her words carefully. She answered, "God, in His wonderful and exciting plan for my life, has given me another of His perfect gifts. And, since all of the gifts of God are good, I have accepted the baptism with the Holy Spirit in the same love as I have accepted the gift of eternal life."

There was a moment of silence, and then came his reply: "Then we won't be able to have you at our church next week, because the meeting just wouldn't have the right spirit."

"Pastor, you must know that Charles and I always respect the teachings of any church we minister in," Frances said. "But we have received many comments that, since the Lord baptized us with the Holy Spirit, people notice much more power in our ministry than it ever had before. We would in no way impose our experience on anyone else without consent from those who invite us to speak. The Holy Spirit is a gentleman. He does not force Himself on anyone who doesn't desire Him."

Her words had no impact upon the pastor, however. His mind was made up before he called, and the conversation was over.

Frances was saddened. She felt sorry for those whose denominational rules and doctrinal traditions were more important than the power of God in their lives. Unfortunately, she would receive several similar calls canceling speaking engagements because of minds closed to the gifts of the Holy Spirit.

Spiritual Growth on Steroids

Following their baptism in the Holy Spirit, Charles and Frances spent every available minute immersing themselves in the written Word of God. The more they read, the more they wanted to read. The more they searched, the more spiritual truths God revealed, which He would use to develop a worldwide healing ministry.

Charles and Frances never obtained seminary degrees to frame and hang on their office walls. In a seminary, the Bible is taught with an understanding of Greek and Hebrew. Charles and Frances studied the Bible with their souls. The Holy Spirit was their teacher. As they ministered, they taught people not how to dissect the Word of God but how to apply it to their lives so that they could draw closer to God, as well as receive the blessings that He had for them.

Charles and Frances taught people not how to dissect the Word of God but how to apply it to their lives so that they could draw closer to God, as well as receive the blessings that He had for them.

The change in their healing ministry was immediate. Before their baptism in the Holy Spirit, they had laid hands on the sick with occasional results. After their baptism, it was not unusual for person after person to exclaim that his or her pain was gone, injured body parts were healed, or that sores and growths had shrunk or disappeared. God taught Charles and Frances that a secret to getting more people healed was to have them do something they could not do before. The Holy Spirit instructed them not to pray for a person but to make a specific command to the particular area of physical need.

God also taught them about demonic spirits. They noticed that the deaf were not being healed as they thought they should. The Lord showed them that a demonic spirit often causes deafness. When they began to command the demonic spirits to leave the deaf individuals, many more were healed than they had experienced previously.

They discovered that, as a general rule, diseases deemed "terminal" by physicians had a demonic spirit involved. They began to command demonic spirits to leave whenever there was a condition that could not be cured by medical science. In doing so, they began to see people healed in large numbers.

For the first time in their ministry, Charles and Frances noticed a flow of power—a tangible energy—coming out of them when they laid hands on people.

For the first time in their ministry, Charles and Frances noticed a flow of power—a tangible energy—coming out of them when they laid hands on people. People fell back or dropped to the floor when they touched them. Sometimes, hundreds of people would fall under the power of the Holy Spirit at once. There were instances when the power of God swept through an auditorium like a mighty rushing wind.

Hunter Ministries in Full Bloom

A wonderful surprise brought great joy to both Charles and Frances. Whereas Charles had formerly been in the background while Frances ministered, he moved into a new dimension after receiving the indwelling of the Holy Spirit.

One time, they were in a meeting in Indiana, Frances was in the forefront as the speaker; Charles, the supportive CPA husband, was standing beside her. Shortly after the service had begun, Charles took the microphone to give his personal testimony, as Frances always asked him to do. As he began to share, the Holy Spirit fell on him, and for the next hour, revelation knowledge flowed out of him. The message was so divinely anointed that even the children in the congregation sat spellbound the entire time.

Behind Charles, there were two chairs. Frances was sitting in one; the other was empty. Frances' mouth showed a joyous smile and her eyes were glued to her husband as he stood before her, speaking under the anointing of God.

After a while, Frances felt the sheer material of her dress sleeve move from a slight breeze as if caused by the motion of someone sitting down in the chair beside her. She assumed the pastor had come up on the stage to ask her when she was going to start speaking. She did not turn to acknowledge him because she didn't want to miss a single word of what Charles was saying. Suddenly, she felt a tug on her sleeve. She turned, expecting to see the pastor—but it was not he. It was Jesus! He was sitting next to her, clearly visible yet transparent. Frances was totally overcome with the presence of God!

Jesus pointed to the bottle of olive oil sitting next to the pulpit. He said, "That is symbolic of the Holy Spirit." Then, He pointed to Charles, saying, "That's the real oil, because the anointing is on him. Let Charles speak tonight."

After almost an hour of speaking, Charles paused and said, "You have come to hear Frances tonight, and I must stop." Frances stepped to the pulpit and told the people what she had just experienced. She said that Charles would be the only speaker that night, in obedience to the direction of the Lord.

From that time forward, Charles was an active and anointed participant in the ministry of the Happy Hunters. Charles and Frances Hunter, together in ministry, became greater than either one of them could have been in ministry alone.

Love without Measure

From the day that Frances Gardner said "I do," she realized that the love that she and Charles had for each other was a divine gift from God. Charles had given her a small manuscript before their marriage that described the last year of his first wife's life, the spiritual growth they had experienced together, and the perfect peace that they received in total surrender to God. After she read it, Frances knew with all of her being that Charles Hunter was a rare type of man, and that he would cover her with devotion, strength, and protection for the rest of her life.

From the day that he met Frances, Charles' only desire was to go everywhere Frances went, to look after her and cherish her, and for them to grow together into the fullness of God's vision for them.

From the day that he met Frances,

Charles' only desire was to go everywhere Frances went, to look after her and cherish her, and for them to grow together into the fullness of God's vision for them. In the last letter Charles wrote to Frances before their wedding, he told Frances that he had asked God to allow him to love her with a love beyond anything he had ever known. His prayer decreed that his wife would be esteemed above all others and all that existed in the natural world.

Wherever the Happy Hunters went, as people were brought into the fullness of God through their ministry, there was always one prominent observation: the quality of love and devotion that they demonstrated for each other. A renowned pastor told them, "Charles and Frances, the way you two love and honor each other, on and off the stage, has probably impacted as many lives as your healing ministry. And you didn't have to say one word."

Chapter Nine

Miracle Ministry

God poured out His Spirit mightily in the 1970s. It was as if God had tired of looking down on sleeping Christianity, and He decided to jostle the church awake. His breath blew across the nation and reached the parched hearts of believers who were frustrated by spiritual stagnation, weary of homiletics, and thirsty for living water.

A secular group marketed a song with the words "God is dead." God must have laughed at the audacity and simply taken it as an opportunity to show the world that He was alive and well, personal and exciting. Charles and Frances were appointed by the Holy Spirit for such a time as this.

For every mainline pastor who called their ministry and canceled an engagement because he thought the Hunters had "gone off the deep end," a dozen others would phone, praying that Charles and Frances would be able to schedule their church into their busy itinerary. Chapters of the Full Gospel Businessmen's Fellowship International, which were flourishing across the nation, called the Hunters from every state. Whenever a banquet hall filled with FGBMFI partners experienced Charles and Frances Hunter, the word spread fast, and Hunter Ministries' phone lines would jam with eager callers.

The First Miracle Service

Pastor Bob Lewis, who led a Southern Baptist congregation in El Paso, Texas, heard Charles and Frances speak at a Full Gospel Businessmen's meeting. He knew that his church needed to experience a move of God and believed that if the Hunters came to El Paso, God would show up at their service. When he called the Hunters, they said they would be able to come to the church in February 1973. Prior to the meeting, the church bulletin announced that Sunday would be a "miracle Sunday." But until the Hunters arrived, a miracle Sunday at that church was one that drew five hundred people.

On Sunday morning, the Southern Baptist congregation learned how to relate to a God who was fabulous. Frances shocked them with her description of a wild sinner who was the center of attention at cocktail parties, successful in business, but lunging through life full steam ahead without a clue as to why she had been placed on this earth. They identified with her pride, her frustration, and her longing to really know a personal savior.

Charles told of his early years living at a high altitude where the fruit would grow wonderfully to a certain point but would never ripen. He shared how God had ripened his heart as the Texas sun ripened delicious fruit. He told how he and Frances had fought and then sought the baptism with the Holy Spirit and how gloriously changed they were after they were filled with the Spirit.

After the Hunters ministered, people were healed, and many fell to the floor under the power of God.

After the Hunters ministered, people flooded the front of the church to be saved and to be baptized in the Holy Spirit. Many were delivered from addictions and bondages that had controlled their lives. People were healed, and many fell to the floor under the power of God. The pastor was thrilled as he witnessed the Spirit of God moving at the end of the service and said to Charles and Frances, "I would love to see the whole front of my church filled with people slain in the spirit."

Charles and Frances ministered again at the evening service and, at the conclusion, went to the back of the auditorium to greet people. They had hardly been seated a minute when they turned to each other simultaneously and asked, "Did God just speak to you?" Charles spoke, and Frances echoed, "God just said to announce a miracle service on Tuesday!"

They were shocked because they had never conducted a miracle service. Charles walked to the front and, after asking the pastor if he could make an announcement, stepped to the microphone and said, "God just told both Frances and me at the same time that we are to have a miracle service on Tuesday night."

Charles turned to Pastor Lewis and asked, "Is that all right?" The pastor nodded, and Charles continued, "Jesus will pass by this church on Tuesday night to heal the sick. Go out and tell your friends to bring the sick, the lame, and the crippled, and He will heal them!"

Pastor Lewis, his wife, and nine-year-old daughter drove Charles and Frances back to their motel after the service. On the way, the Hunters shared how the baptism with the Holy Spirit had impacted their study of the Bible, their understanding and discernment of spiritual things, and the anointing of God on their ministry. When they got to the motel, the Lewises were anxious to receive the baptism and followed Charles and Frances into their motel room. A little while later, all three came out rejoicing and speaking in tongues.

When they arrived home, their twenty-year-old daughter immediately knew that something had happened to them, and she wanted it, too. The next morning at breakfast, she asked Charles and Frances to lay hands on her, and she was baptized in the Holy Spirit right there in the restaurant. The last child, nineteen-year-old Bob Jr., was reluctant and kept silent.

It's Just a Little Demon

When Tuesday evening arrived, the pastor introduced Charles and Frances to a young lady named Mary. As they extended their hands to greet her, she ran from them, screaming. The Hunters knew in their spirits that it was not the woman who was upset but the demonic spirit residing within her. They had publicly announced a miracle service, and now the enemy was creating a diversion by bringing a demon-possessed woman into the place.

Charles turned to the pastor and said, "We'll start the service. You bind Satan by the power of God's Holy Spirit and command the demon to come out, in the name of Jesus." The pastor and his wife, who had been filled with the Holy Spirit less than forty-eight hours earlier, took Mary into the church office, and Charles and Frances started the service.

Midway through the service, Bob Jr. and his sister were called out of the service and into their father's office. Near the end of the service, they returned to the auditorium. Charles and Frances called Bob Jr. forward, asking him to come to the microphone and tell the crowd what had happened. Bob Jr., who had stuttered all his life, stepped forward and, in halting words, told the sweet little group of Southern Baptists, who had never heard of active demons until that day, that his parents had cast a devil out of Mary and that she had been saved!

God Has His Way

When Bob Jr. had finished, Charles spoke to him, saying, "Bob, Jesus would like to heal your stuttering. Is that okay?"

Bob promptly said, "Yes."

Charles placed his hands on the young man. He prayed and asked the Lord to do a miracle in his life, to go back in time to the moment he was conceived and remove anything that might have frightened or disturbed him, to remove anything that could have made him feel insecure or inferior. He asked that Bob be completely healed, in the name of Jesus. Then Charles instructed him, "Say, 'Thank You, Jesus!'"

With no hesitation, Bob said, "Thank You, Jesus!"

Charles smiled broadly and asked, "What happened to you?"

Bob turned to the congregation and spoke with perfect enunciation, "As Charles prayed for me, the power of God was so great that I could hardly stand up! Most of you know that I have always stuttered. But now I am healed!"

"Jesus is passing by this Baptist church tonight, and He is willing to touch the life of anyone, either spiritually or physically."

Bob read four verses from the Bible without faltering in his speech, and the church erupted with applause and praise!

Charles faced the congregation and told them, "Jesus is passing by this

Baptist church tonight, and He is willing to touch the life of anyone, either spiritually or physically."

Faith was ignited in the crowd, and people began to come forward for healing. An eleven-year-old deaf girl whose mother was working in the nursery was healed. A friend of her mother's ran down the hall shouting about what the Lord had done. The girl's mother ran through the hall toward the auditorium calling her daughter's name, and when she reached her daughter, the little girl heard her mother's voice for the first time!

Another little girl was healed of cerebral palsy. When asked what had happened to her, she replied, "Jesus walked by and touched me!" The Hunters rejoiced as they learned the rest of her story.

That morning, a little boy had been in the service when Charles had announced that Jesus would pass by that night. He stopped by the home of this little girl with cerebral palsy and told her mother that she needed to take her daughter to the service that night, because Jesus was going to pass by there and heal people.

The girl's mother scoffed, "Jesus isn't coming by that church!" And she refused to take her daughter to the service.

The boy believed without a doubt that his little friend would be healed if Jesus touched her. So, even though he was only about ten years old, he carried her on his back to the church.

The little girl now stood before Charles and Frances. Charles smiled at her, leaned over, and asked her if she thought she could walk. She took one shaky step and then, slowly, took another step. Soon, she was running around the auditorium. Within two days, she was playing on the playground with her friends for the first time in her life!

A whole congregation recognized that Jesus was in their midst, and they began to reach out for more of Him.

A whole congregation of Southern Baptists rejoiced before God. They recognized that Jesus was in their midst, and they began to reach out for more of Him. The wife of the chairman of the deacons' board was filled with the Holy Spirit and spoke in tongues. Bob Jr., no longer reluctant, was baptized with the Holy Spirit. People came forward for prayer and, as the pastor had desired, the altar was crowded with people slain in the Spirit.

They tried to dismiss the service at 10:15, but it was well after midnight before the people left the church. Charles and Frances marveled at the outpouring of God's miracle-working power. They knew that the Baptist church would never be the same again, and they knew that they would never be the same again. In fact, they felt like they could have flown from El Paso back to Houston without an airplane!

A Spiritual Earthquake for the Quakers

One day, Frances excitedly told Charles, "We just got invited to speak at an annual Meeting of Friends in Des Moines, Iowa. It's a big event every year that Quakers come to from all over the country, and they want us to speak on the power of the Holy Spirit!"

"Hallelujah!" Charles replied. "God is pouring out His Spirit on all flesh!"

As they considered whether to include teaching on speaking in tongues, they received a letter from the coordinator of the event saying that she had just been baptized in the Holy Spirit. Before the Hunters arrived in Des Moines, the woman's husband had also been filled with the Holy Spirit. God was moving among the Quakers!

The first service was on a Friday morning, and it did not have the results that Charles and Frances had anticipated. On Saturday morning, Frances asked God what they should do to fire up the congregation. God told her, "Tell the people that tonight I will touch them in a miraculous way."

Frances was obedient and told the congregation, "God just told me that tonight there is going to be a miracle service. Be sure that you're here and that you bring anyone who needs healing or a miracle from God. In fact, if anyone needs to leave right now, you go ahead and call everyone you know so they can have time to get here tonight!"

After the words came out of her mouth, Frances' heart raced as she thought, *I'm really confident that I heard God, but I can't believe I just said that. Well, either God is going to show up, or I missed it!*

That night, after she and Charles talked about God's will for healing, Frances could hardly wait for the Quakers to experience the power of God! She beckoned to the group and enthusiastically invited everyone who needed healing to line up on the right side of the auditorium. But not one person came!

The people had never been to a healing service before, so they had no idea what to expect, and no one wanted to be the first to step forward. Finally, one woman stepped forward. Frances silently asked God if she had heard Him correctly that morning. God responded by directing her to lay hands on a nearby pastor.

She and Charles motioned for the pastor to step toward them. Charles laid hands on him, and he fell to the floor. His wife screamed from the audience. She had never seen anything like it and didn't know if her husband was hurt or what was going on. Then, Charles and Frances asked her to come forward. She bravely obeyed, even though her husband was still lying on the floor, apparently unconscious. Something inside her gave her a sense of peace, as well as a desire to accept this, if it was of God. They laid hands on her, and she plopped down right beside her husband. Thirty minutes later, the pastor crawled over to his chair, so drunk in the Spirit that he had to pull himself onto the chair; even then, he could barely keep from sliding off of it.

As soon as the pastor and his wife were slain in the Spirit, the line for healing grew to twenty and then to fifty. An older man who was deaf and blind came forward. His hearing was restored immediately, but not his sight. Two days later, Charles and Frances received word that he had been sitting in his home, and as his wife walked by, he had commented on her beautiful smile. His eyesight had gloriously returned!

He Sets My Feet a-Dancing

Charles and Frances were invited to a Chinese church in the Houston area for a celebration of praise. When the choir began singing, they were shocked to see feet thumping and legs poking out from under the choir robes. Frances pulled her Bible up to cover her face because she could not keep from laughing. She thought, *They can't be dancing! You don't dance in church!*

She finally put down the Bible and studied the faces of the people who were dancing. All the people looked as if they had just opened their best birthday presents. Their faces were radiant with joy as they offered their whole bodies to God in praise. Frances had never seen people so expressive of their love for the Lord.

On the way home, Charles and Frances decided that dancing before the Lord was not bad if it was a means of demonstrating one's love and appreciation for God and all of His goodness. So, they went home, shut the door to their bedroom, closed all the blinds, and Charles Hunter began to learn how to dance before the Lord! He did not have great coordination, though, because he had never danced in his life. His sense of rhythm was very creative, to put it nicely, but his persistence and determination were commendable. While Frances lay in bed encouraging him, he danced all over their bedroom and discovered how to express his tremendous love for the Lord in an even fuller way!

Charles became known as the Arthur Murray of the charismatic world!

From then on, when the worship began in a church service, Charles would always lead in the dancing. He became known as the Arthur Murray of the charismatic world!

Lifelong Bonds and Friendships

Word about the Happy Hunters' healing and miracle ministry spread rapidly. Several Christian television networks had been started that regularly featured ministries that were impacting the nation. The Hunters were in high demand to make appearances on Pat Robertson's *700 Club* and became favorites on Jim and Tammy Bakker's *PTL Club*. The viewing audience for these programs numbered in the millions.

God also arranged divine contacts for the Hunters that brought both international credibility to their ministry and valued friendships with leaders who would provide encouragement and support for many years to come.

Dr. Lester Sumrall identified strongly with the Hunters because, like they did, he believed that "with God, anything is possible." He took God at His word and recognized that quality in Charles and Frances. After they had become friends, he invited them to go to the Philippines to minister with him. He was always available with wise advice and kind guidance whenever they asked for it.

When Dr. Sumrall received a vision from God that challenged him to feed the hungry around the world, he held a telethon to raise money and asked the Hunters if they would come and lead a portion of the telethon for him. When they showed up in South Bend, Indiana, the telethon had been in full swing for a few days, and Dr. Sumrall had been before the camera almost nonstop. When Charles and Frances arrived, Dr. Sumrall left the stage to go and rest. They ran the telethon for many hours and were able to help him build the financial support the ministry needed. When he asked later what their fee was, they replied, "Nothing!" Other well-known evangelists had charged thousands of dollars, which diminished the much-needed funds for the hungry, so when the Hunters said they wanted absolutely nothing, Dr. Sumrall wept. He remained a close friend and spiritual brother until his death in 1996.

Frances and Charles drew the attention of a pastor and his wife in Denver, Colorado, who were struggling to build their church. To raise funds, Wally and Marilyn Hickey had invited a nationally known speaker to come and lead a fund-raising event. The event was not as successful as they had hoped, however, and the speaker required a large honorarium. With that and the additional expenses of the event, the new church ended up with a debt of eighteen thousand dollars.

Not sure of what to do, Marilyn called Frances and asked if she could help them. Charles and Frances flew to Denver and held services all weekend. When the last offering was counted, they had just over the eighteen thousand dollars needed to pay off the debt. The Hunters and the Hickeys have remained close friends for more than thirty years.

Each time the Hunters spoke in a church, held a miracle service, appeared on television, or talked with people in airports or on the streets, they conveyed an enthusiasm for the things of God that defied description. Love poured from them and built bonds that remained for a lifetime. Their friendships were among great and small alike, and thousands would come to describe them as the most loving and the most loved evangelists in the nation.

The Hunters conveyed an enthusiasm for the things of God that defied description.

Chapter Ten

Worldwide Healing Explosions

> *You are to go into all the world and preach the Good News to everyone, everywhere. Those who believe and are baptized will be saved. But those who refuse to believe will be condemned. And those who believe shall use my authority to cast out demons, and they shall speak new languages. They will be able even to handle snakes with safety, and if they drink anything poisonous, it won't hurt them; and they will be able to place their hands on the sick and heal them.* (Mark 16:15–18 TLB)

Charles and Frances accepted the Great Commission without reservation. People flocked to their meetings from every town within driving distance, and there were many who traveled by plane to their miracle services because they believed with all their hearts, "If the Hunters lay hands on me, I will be healed."

The Hunters did not accept invitations only from large churches or conventions. They ministered in school auditoriums and dingy theaters in small towns because of their passion to do the work of Jesus and their desire to be available to as many people as possible so that they could receive healing. Their schedule was often grueling, so they learned to take afternoon naps whenever possible. Whenever they walked onto the platform, they radiated love, energy, and excitement about what God was going to do during that meeting.

A Vision for the World

The more Charles and Frances studied the Bible, the more strongly they believed that if God could use a couple in their sixties—whose backgrounds were a wild sinner and a dried-up spiritual prune—to preach the gospel, cast out demons, and heal the sick, He could use any believer.

Everywhere they ministered, the Hunters began to call people from the congregation to come up and lay hands on the sick.

Since Jesus talked to believers about continuing His works and doing even greater works, the Hunters knew that they were to talk to believers just as Jesus had done. Everywhere they ministered, they began to call people from the congregation to come up and lay hands on the sick. In many cases, they asked someone who had just been healed to lay hands on the next person, and that person would be healed!

In order to give more thorough instruction to believers, the Hunters built the City of Light Bible School next door to their ministry offices. It was not long before they realized that the building was limited, the hands-on application was limited, and the ultimate outreach was limited. What they had done was good, and many lives were changed, but God had a bigger plan.

In June 1980, the Lord visited Frances in a vision that gave her insight into God's enlarging plan for their ministry. Frances saw the world with silver and gold bands covering the entire planet, but not in the orderly arrangement of lines on a globe. These bands spilled all over the world like melted silver and gold rivulets running down mountains and into valleys. Some were wide, some were narrow, others looked like large blobs of melted silver or gold. Then, she saw people begin to rise up and stand on these irregular patterns of liquid silver and gold.

Frances shared the vision with Charles, and together they asked God to show them what the vision meant. It became clear that the Lord was telling them to take the total message of salvation, which included healing, to the entire world. They were to multiply themselves by teaching the masses how to operate in the supernatural, resulting in a glorious, global network of believers healing the sick.

They were willing and ready to do anything that God asked of them, but the entire world was a fairly large project, and there were just two of them. "God, how can we go into every little nook and cranny of the world to teach people how to heal the sick?" Frances asked.

The Vision Becomes Reality

As Charles and Frances were faithful to continue doing what they knew to do, God revealed to them a phenomenal method of multiplication. The newly invented VCR had appeared almost overnight in nearly every home in the nation. People had videotapes stacked on bookshelves, in closets, and on end tables, and many people made their own recordings with camcorders. It was popular for parents to film home videos of their children to send to grandparents and other relatives who lived far away or simply to keep for posterity.

It was so obvious! The Hunters saw how they could teach students of every nationality and language through video schools. The videotapes would put Charles and Frances and their entire healing seminar into tiny boxes that could be shipped easily to any place in the world. The Hunters would reach students they would never meet, and what God had taught them would change lives in remote areas all over the world. They immediately scheduled an experienced video technician to tape a twelve-hour training series that they entitled *How to Heal the Sick.*

In it, they discussed and demonstrated the methods that Jesus, Peter, and Paul used to heal the sick, as well as what they had learned through their own experiences in ministering to thousands of people. One of the keys that the Holy Spirit pointed out to them was that Jesus did not pray for the sick; He touched, spoke, and commanded. When they began to lay hands on people and make specific commands by the power of the Holy Spirit in the name of Jesus, the healings increased dramatically. They had also learned that a key to people receiving healing was telling them to do something they could not do before.

Jesus did not pray for the sick; He touched, spoke, and commanded.

There were so many things they could now share with such ease! The video schools could be played in churches, homes, and virtually anywhere else with the proper technology. They could be played multiple times to the same group or passed on to others. Could the video healing schools fulfill the vision God had given Frances of the globe covered with a network of precious silver and gold strands?

The Monday after the twelve-hour video set was complete and a stack of copies had been produced, God sent a missionary to Paris, the City of Light, who knew nothing of the video training program. Charles and Frances brimmed with excitement as they placed the brand-new videotape series, *How to Heal the Sick*, in his hands.

On Tuesday, another missionary arrived, and they gave him the video set. He called them two weeks later to report that, once back in Tanzania, he had rented a building that could hold three hundred people. He had placed one small advertisement in the newspaper and, on the night of the training, had to turn away crowds of people. He could hardly wait to call the ministry and report that a number of people were healed as they watched the tapes, plus many salvations.

In the next three months, video healing schools started in Peru, Bolivia, the Philippines, as well as in three additional countries in Africa. Copies of the videotapes began to be recorded in various languages, making it easy for nationals to understand and build faith without requiring a translator.

The Praise and the Controversy

In 1981, Charles and Frances wrote their book, *How to Heal the Sick*, which became a best seller and has been translated into 80 percent of the world's major languages. Churches, home fellowships, and individuals began using the videotapes and books together to have healing schools. The Hunters received phone calls and letters from all over the U.S. and other nations that provided testimonies of healings and miracles that had taken place because of the healing schools. The faith of believers that had been locked up for generations by tradition had been unleashed as God honored ordinary people obeying the Great Commission.

With the jubilation, though, came criticism. While invitations increased for the Hunters to hold miracle services, skeptics openly scorned them for proclaiming that they could teach a believer how to heal the sick.

Of course, many of the skeptics did not believe in divine healing. Others claimed that God can heal when it is His will, but all a believer can do is pray and hope because sometimes it is God's will and sometimes it isn't.

The Hunters were too busy to be affected by negative opinions. As a young girl, Frances had learned to turn criticism into a positive force, and she considered opposition merely a challenge. Charles had developed a tenacity that propelled him forward to reach every goal he ever set for his life. When many people of their age were retiring after lifetimes of doing little, if anything, for the Lord, Charles and Frances continued to move forward, believing in God for even more excitement and victories while serving Him.

The thousands of people who were healed leapt with joy, removed their braces, and rejoiced as cancerous growths disappeared. The power of God had touched them, and they simply gave God all the glory, as did Charles and Frances.

The thousands of people who were healed leapt with joy, removed their braces, and rejoiced as cancerous growths disappeared.

The First Healing Explosion

In November 1984, Charles and Frances were guests on a Christian television program hosted by Russ Bixler, president of Pittsburgh's Channel 40. While on the air, he said to them, "I think you ought to hold a healing seminar on television to teach the people how to heal the sick. If you will come and do a healing seminar, we will assist you in scheduling a meeting to help with your expenses."

The Hunters returned to Houston and communicated with Russ several times without finding a date that would work for both the television station and them. Finally, Russ called and said, "I believe God wants you to come to Pittsburgh for a healing seminar the week of July 4 and follow it with a miracle service at the Civic Arena [now Mellon Arena] on Independence Day." The date suited them perfectly.

Charles and Frances had never held a meeting in a venue of that size. As they realized the great potential of what God could do in the Pittsburgh arena, they began pouring their energy into the preparations.

They immediately contacted churches and partners all over the nation. Their goal was to have one hundred and twenty healing teams and two hundred and forty people trained by their *How to Heal the Sick* videotapes and books. The Hunters would come to Pittsburgh three days before the meeting to hold final training sessions with the teams. On the night of the event, the teams would be the ones laying hands on the sick—not the Hunters.

They had passionately preached that "if Charles and Frances can do it, you can do it, too!" and had trained a few at a time with successful results. But the July meeting would be the first time that the Hunters would actually turn over the entire miracle service to a host of ordinary believers who had been trained to heal the sick. They anticipated an explosion of the power of God throughout the arena and decided to advertise the event as a "Healing Explosion."

The Hunters anticipated an explosion of the power of God throughout the arena and decided to advertise the event as a "Healing Explosion."

In the back of Frances' mind was the word from the Lord that had come long ago as she and Charles moved their home Bible study to a 1,200-seat auditorium. She and Charles knew that this first Healing Explosion would lead them to the fulfillment of God's promise that they would one day minister in the Astrodome.

Prayer Backing and Awesome Results

When they sent out a request for prayer warriors, people responded from all over the world. They prayed for the multitude of tasks in the natural that needed to be performed. They prayed for finances—the Hunters would be spending more for this one meeting than they had spent in the history of their ministry. Prayers went up for all the people who would be coming into the city needing salvation or healing. Loving, intercessory prayer covered the Hunters, who asked God for wisdom, strength, and spiritual power so that they could lead the people as He would have them to do.

Excitement grew among the Christian community. Joe Horst, a Pittsburgh pubic relations expert, called to volunteer wherever he was needed, and Frances said, "Great! You can be the coordinator!" Nationally known praise and worship leader Rick Cook volunteered to lead worship for the Explosion. Ron Kite, who had developed the supportive ministries for mega-church Victory Christian Center of Tulsa, Oklahoma, coordinated all the ushers, greeters, and security personnel for the event. He would later negotiate with large arenas throughout the nation for scores of Healing Explosions.

Church leaders from a hundred-mile area met for prayer breakfasts in a spirit of unprecedented unity. Choirs began to practice together, crossing denominational lines. Anywhere there was a need relative to the Explosion, God urged people to offer their talents and time.

Anywhere there was a need relative to the Explosion, God urged people to offer their talents and time.

Charles and Frances' vision for one hundred and twenty healing teams proved to be too small. More than one thousand believers fulfilled the Hunters' requirement of viewing the twelve-hour *How to Heal the Sick* videos along with studying the book. They drove or flew into Pittsburgh three days before the meeting to participate in live training with the Hunters. Doctors and chiropractors arrived, as well, to appear on a panel to explain how various illnesses and injuries affected the body and how to minister specifically, in the power of God, to get the body divinely healed.

The Explosion!

Months before the Healing Explosion, Charles and Frances had flown to Pittsburgh to share the vision at the charismatic conference that was held at Duquesne University, a college situated on a hilltop overlooking the beautiful dome of the Civic Arena. As the audience stood and directed their hands toward the dome to pray, giant angels suddenly appeared all around the dome.

The Hunters thrilled at the sight and believed that the angels, who were standing on the lip of the dome and stretching their arms all the way to the top, were assigned to protect it and set it apart for God's glory and power on July 4. Reports came to the Hunters from many others who had seen this phenomenon. Each time the Hunters flew to Pittsburgh for radio or TV appearances, they saw the angels, and at every Healing Explosion, whether in the United States or abroad, angels were always sighted above, around, or in the coliseum or stadium.

On the afternoon of July 4, 1985, eleven thousand excited people flocked to the Civic Arena to get settled into their seats. The choir members made their ways to a section reserved for them. Over one thousand healing team members sat throughout the arena, their expectancy level almost beyond containment. Many people wept as they sensed the electrifying power of God all around them. At two o'clock, the worship service began, and the anointing of the Holy Spirit intensified as praises filled the great arena for over an hour.

Charles and Frances stepped up to the podium as servants of the God whom they loved with all of their being. They were not there to preach an eloquent message or to build their ministry. They had come in simple obedience to the passion God had placed in their hearts to train His people to win the lost to Jesus, to lead them in the baptism with the Holy Spirit, and to lay hands on the sick so that they would recover.

Frances led the entire assembly in a prayer of salvation so that every person there would have the opportunity to receive Jesus as Lord and Savior before the Explosion went any further. Then, Charles ministered the baptism with the Holy Spirit. Over five thousand people stood up and walked down to fill the area in front of the platform. As they began to speak in their heavenly prayer languages, the entire crowd joined them, and the building resounded with the mighty chorus.

The seats emptied when Frances called for every person who wanted to be healed or who needed a miracle to get up.

When everyone had returned to their seats, the healing team members, well-prepared for their mission, rose to their feet. At Frances' cue, they moved in long, flowing lines as extensions of the arms of God down to the arena floor.

Frances called for every person who wanted to be healed or who needed a miracle to get up and make his or her way to one of the healing teams spread around the arena.

The seats seemed to empty as people streamed forward to receive a touch from God. Lines of patient people formed around the healing teams, and voices of faith and expectancy reached the throne of God. Some people were healed before they had even reached the team who would minister to them.

Many of the healing teams consisted of children who had gone through the training with their parents. Age, size, and color had no bearing on either the teams or those coming to them. Everyone knew that God was in the arena and that He was going to touch, heal, and deliver through the hands of His servants without distinction.

Charles and Frances could not keep the tears from welling in their eyes. They watched, enraptured, as the vision that had been in their hearts for over a decade played out before them.

Those with testimonies began to form lines at either end of the stage. One woman in line had come in a wheelchair. Several children had gone over to her and laid hands on her, commanding her in the name of Jesus to get up and walk. She walked to the stage, unassisted, and rejoiced that her body was no longer stiff and in pain from crippling arthritis.

A man who had suffered from black lung began to breathe normally. Someone with a shoe that was built up two inches left with both legs the same length. He laughed because he needed to go shopping for new shoes right away!

A ninety-one-year-old woman came with hearing aids in both ears. After the healing team ministered to her, she was able to hear someone whisper behind her.

"Mother, look at my nose!" exclaimed a small girl. Her mother gasped as she saw the child's formerly crooked nose looking perfectly symmetrical and beautiful.

A man whose eyes could distinguish only between light and dark could count the healing team members' fingers after hands were laid on him.

Crossed eyes were straightened by the power of God, ulcers disappeared, and some

Crossed eyes were straightened by the power of God, ulcers disappeared, and some people just released all their emotional pain to the Lord and received peace.

people just released all their emotional pain to the Lord and received peace.

A Jewish mother was in the crowd, watching as her Christian daughter ministered with the healing teams. At a dinner party the next day, this woman testified before all of her family members to the miracles she had seen performed in the name of Jesus. She excitedly told of deaf ears opening, blind eyes seeing, and lame people walking out of wheelchairs. A few days later, as her daughter boarded a plane to return home, the mother held out her hand, three fingers of which had been withered for many years with painful arthritis. She asked, "Do you think Jesus could do something about this?" The Messiah healed her fingers on the spot, and she embraced her daughter with a new understanding of Jesus.

By seven o'clock that evening, the arena was deserted except for a couple who wandered in thinking the Explosion started at seven o'clock. The last healing team prayed for them before they left, rejoicing. As workers came in to prepare the building for the next event, they saw discarded hearing aids, crutches, leg braces, foot braces, and other signs of what God had done on Independence Day in Pittsburgh.

Second Healing Explosion held at the Carpenters' home church in Lakeland, FL.

The Explosions Go Worldwide

If it could have been viewed on a spiritual map, the city of Pittsburgh would have radiated a supernatural glow that day. Heaven surely rejoiced, as did eleven thousand believers whose lives were powerfully affected. Testimonies continued to come in to the Hunters of healings documented by doctors' examinations, X-rays, and blood tests. Lumps and cancers were gone, cases of diabetes had been healed, and broken bones had even been knit back together.

Testimonies continued to come in to the Hunters of healings documented by doctors' examinations, X-rays, and blood tests.

Over a thousand reports came in of new ministries birthed that day as believers either witnessed or experienced firsthand what God wanted to do—and would do—through ordinary believers.

The Pittsburgh Healing Explosion was just the first of more than a hundred Healing Explosions that would take place over the next five years. The Hunters rented the largest arenas available in major cities coast-to-coast, including Lakeland, Denver, Anaheim, Chicago, Fargo, Hartford, Minneapolis, Cleveland, Kansas City, and Anchorage. Their agenda enabled them to hold one large Healing Explosion per month, with one or more smaller ones in between.

At the same time, they managed to hold Healing Explosions in Colombia, the Philippines, South Africa, Brazil, Holland, Ireland, Ukraine, Guatemala, El Salvador, Uruguay, Argentina, and Taiwan. The Hunters ministered in forty-nine nations, including those in which they had ministered prior to the Healing Explosions. They visited some nations more than once, and often they would go from city to city within one nation.

Most of the international Healing Explosions were held in outdoor stadiums, some with crowds of more than sixty thousand filling both the bleachers and the athletic field. Some of the events had as many as four thousand healing team members, who were trained to minister confidently to the sick.

The miracles overseas seemed even more spectacular than those in the United States. More blind eyes were opened, more deaf people

One hundred people came out of wheelchairs in Bogota, Columbia.

received hearing, more harmful growths disappeared, and more crippled people regained full mobility. At one service in Bogotá, Colombia, over a hundred people came out of their wheelchairs and stretchers or dropped their crutches. At a service in Brazil, scores of wheelchairs were passed to the front of the stadium, and one man who had been paralyzed from the waist down in a terrible car wreck ran the circumference of the hockey field. He made his way to the stage and shouted, "I'm not even a Christian, and God healed me! Please, I want to be a Christian!"

For too long, many have felt that only the "stars"—the evangelists, the apostles, the prophets—could do the healing, and yet before our eyes we have witnessed miracles and healings taking place through the obedience of people like Tom, Abby, Stephanie, and Jim—ordinary people who were not content sitting on their church pews. Every day of our lives, we praise God that He commissioned us to teach believers that "If Charles and Frances can do it, you can do it, too!"[6]

[6] Charles and Frances Hunter, *Miracles, Miracles, Miracles* (Kingwood, TX: Hunter Books, 2008), 37.

Chapter Eleven

Holy Laughter

"How can you be unhappy when you're saved?" Frances had asked a woeful-looking Christian woman. She was sharing the story with the congregation of a church in Austin, Texas.

She opened her Bible and began to read: *"For the kingdom of God is not eating and drinking, but righteousness and peace and joy in the Holy Spirit"* (Romans 14:17). *"These things I have spoken to you, that My joy may remain in you, and that your joy may be full"* (John 15:11).

Frances continued, "John 16:22 is a verse that I just discovered! It says that '*no one will take away your joy*' (NIV). Isn't that absolutely incredible, that there is nothing in this entire world that can take away the joy that God has given you? My joy started the day I got saved! I realized the wild sinner that I was and that God instantly forgave me in the twinkling of an eye and that everything that I had ever done had been totally forgiven and forgotten! I remember writing in one of my Bibles, 'If You can't remember it, I can't remember it, either!' Hallelujah!"

Frances and Charles were ministering on holy laughter for Pastor Lee Boss and his wife, Sue. The pastor and his wife knew Frances to be a master storyteller who shared hilarious anecdotes whenever she ministered. The church always burst forth in laughter when Frances related her "getting saved" or "getting filled with the Holy Spirit" stories.

The Bosses also knew that Frances used humor to reach people with the truths that she was teaching, and that laughter would cause them to remember what they had been taught. Tonight, she was assuring them that there was a new wave of the Holy Spirit moving in the body of Christ, and that, through laughter, God was giving mighty breakthroughs and manifestations of His power.

Frances decided to tell the audience how she first fell under the power of the Holy Spirit at Kathryn Kuhlman's meeting at the First Presbyterian Church of Pittsburgh.

"Kathryn stepped off the stage, and you know, that's a horrible feeling for people because there are some of them out there saying, 'Touch me!' And others are saying, 'Don't you dare come close to me!' I was in that second group—'Don't you dare come close to me!'

"She came to the second row, and I was so glad she turned the other way because there was a friend there. He got up—and he wasn't sick at all—and she just said, 'Jesus, bless my brother,' and he fell down!

"I thought, *How come he fell down? He didn't even get healed! I know; she is electrically charged! She has some kind of a battery up her long sleeve! And she has something in her hand, and she just goes zap and puts a little charge on it, and they get shocked!*

"So I thought, *I will take a real good look and see what is going on.* I was looking at this man on the floor who looked so perfectly happy lying there. I stared at her feet, and my eyes slowly moved up, up, up, and when they got high enough, I saw her hand. I was sitting on the second row, the second person in, and her finger was beckoning. She had the longest finger I have ever seen in my entire life! I never saw anybody with a finger that long, and it was directed right at me!

Frances said, "God, if this is of You, let me see what it is."

"I took a look at her, and for those of you who have seen her, you know she is very skinny. I thought, *I am twice as big as you are! No way can you push me over!* But something on the inside of me said, *God, if this is of You, let me see what it is.*

"Be careful, be careful, be careful what you say to God! I stepped out in the aisle, knowing I was twice as big as Kathryn Kuhlman, and she said, 'Jesus, bless my sister!'

"How many of you know what happened to me? Flat out! I didn't even know she touched me! I was flat on the floor! And they had a marble floor in the Presbyterian church! I was going to speak at a Christian women's club after that, and I had on my best dress, and now here I am rolling on the floor in my dress just wiping up all the dust in the Presbyterian Church! I could have cared less! Hallelujah!"

The Bosses and their congregation roared with laughter. Frances paused long enough to let them get their breaths, then went on to tell of an experience that happened shortly after she and Charles were baptized in the Holy Spirit.

"We went to a Full Gospel Businessmen's Fellowship meeting in Houston. We had gotten over the barriers of a few things by this time, so we went there, and after the service, I noticed that one of the men, when he laid hands on the people, made them fall down. I didn't even know what it was, so I went over to him real quick. I am amazed at the boldness that I have sometimes! I said to him, 'How do you do that?'

"He said, 'Why do you want to know?'

"I said, 'Well, because I fell down at a Kathryn Kuhlman service and I want my husband to fall down. I believe in spiritual equality. I believe a man and wife ought to stay on the same spiritual level, as closely as they can, so now that I have fallen down and cleaned up the floor, I want Charles to fall down!'

"He asked, 'You want your husband to fall down?'

"I said, 'Yes, I want my husband to fall down.'

"He asked, 'Where is he?' I went and got Charles, and then the man asked, 'This is Charles?'

"I said, 'Yes.'

"He asked, 'You want him to fall down?'

"I said, 'I want him to fall down.'

"He said, 'Stand beside him.'

"So I stood beside him, and I am just looking at Charles and I knew he was going to get the old One! Two! Boom! I just knew he was going to get it, so I'm looking at Charles, and the man said, 'Jesus, bless my sister!'

"Boom! I was flat on the floor. It was Charles I wanted to fall down! I didn't want to fall down again, but I went down! And one second later, Charles followed me, down on the floor. It was special, because that man held our hands together, and he said, 'I separate you for special service unto the Lord.'

"It was a moment I will never forget. Then Charles got up, and I couldn't! Somebody had poured Elmer's glue on that carpet! I was stuck as tight as anything you ever saw in your entire life! I'd never heard of anything like this, and I was stuck! I couldn't get my feet, I couldn't get my arms, I couldn't get my head, I couldn't get anything out of that Elmer's glue on the floor! I struggled and struggled and struggled and I couldn't get up. I was lying in the midst of, you know, the desserts that they drop on floors. I had a beautiful, long, chiffon dress on, just lying on all this cherry cobbler and chocolate pudding and all that kind of stuff, and I'm doing my best to get up off the floor, and I can't get up off the floor!

"And the most unusual thing happened to my stomach! All of a sudden, I felt like somebody had given me a divine Alka-Seltzer and it was right in the middle of my belly, if you want to call it that. I felt this Alka-Seltzer that bubbled, and it bubbled, and it bubbled, and it bubbled, and it kept getting higher and higher, and I began to panic. And I thought, *I am going to laugh. As sure as anything, I am going to laugh.*

"Suddenly, the Alka-Seltzer got up to here, then it got up to here, and when it got there, I knew that I was lost. I put my hand over my mouth, and I did everything I could to stop laughing, but I couldn't stop it!

"When the Holy Ghost drops laughter on you, there is absolutely nothing that you can do about it!"

"When the Holy Ghost drops laughter on you, there is absolutely nothing that you can do about it! I mean, I just laughed and laughed and laughed, and it wasn't a ladylike laugh at all! I mean, it wasn't a little 'Tee hee, tee hee.' It was 'HA, HA, HA, HA, HA, HA!' It was so loud and so unladylike that I am glad I am dead to self or I would have been embarrassed to no end! The only thing that I could think about was, *I must be excited about Charles' falling down,* because I never laughed like that in my entire life! I couldn't shut up! I absolutely could not shut up!

"I must have laughed for thirty minutes, and then I thought, *Well, I really made a spectacle of myself! They will never ask me to come back again!* Finally, the Elmer's glue wore off and somebody came over and picked me up off of the floor. I sat down very quietly the rest of the evening because I thought I had really done enough for that night!

"Well, I forgot about this. Nobody asked, 'Why did you laugh?' Nobody told me what it was. Nobody explained anything to me, so I just sort of put it in the back recesses of my mind and never thought about it until some years later.

"Maybe about a year after that, I was reminded of it very gently because we were in a service in the State of Washington. Now, at that time—this was twenty-three years ago—people did not fall under the power the way they do today. Today, people with ministries of all kinds just raise their hands and people fall under the power of God, but at that time, about the only time it ever happened was in the Kathryn Kuhlman services.

"One night, in one of our services, I made the mistake that I have never made since then: I closed my eyes when I prayed. I was praying for this man who kept getting shorter and shorter. I kept my eyes shut, and he disappeared! I remember I was feeling around all over for him, and I couldn't find him anyplace.

"Finally, I opened one eye, thinking God would never notice, and I opened one eye, and the man was lying on the floor! I thought, *I've killed him! He must have really been sick, and my prayer was too long, and I just plain killed him!* That is why I don't shut my eyes when I pray. I look at you because I want to see what happens!

"Then, we went to the service in Washington, and we had somebody come up, and the person got healed. We laid hands on him, and he fell under the power of God, and everybody in the audience gasped. You can always tell when an audience has never seen anything like that.

"I asked, 'How many of you have never seen anybody fall under the power of God?' I would say at least 95 percent of the audience raised their hands. So the Spirit of God spoke and said, 'Get twenty of them up here.'

"We picked out two rows of people, regardless of who they were, and asked them to line up. Charles and I went down the line and just said, 'Jesus, bless them. Jesus, bless them. Jesus, bless them.' Every one of them fell under the power of God! But there was Elmer's glue that night, too! They were stuck on the floor! They couldn't get up!

"Remember, we were very new in Pentecost. When you are new in Pentecost, there are a lot of things you don't understand, so we thought, *What did we do wrong there? We'll lead the praise and worship.* If you have ever heard either one of us sing, you know that we are the world's worst singers. Both of us have flat voices. We were up there just trying to lead them in some more singing, and they were trying to drown us out, so we sang real loud. These people are still lying on the floor, and finally the lady that was third in suddenly rolled over on her side and started laughing and beating on the floor!

"Now, Charles and I were taught that everything must be done 'decently and in order.' So, we went off that side of the stage because we were going to quiet this down, whatever this was. It wasn't very decent and in order. But before we got off the side of the stage and to her, she got up, took off like a shot, ran over to a chair, and began beating on a woman with both hands! I mean, just beating on her!

"Charles and I were horrified! I thought there was going to be a riot! I thought they were going to call the police or something like that, so the two of us ran over there as fast as we could because we were going to stop whatever this nonsense was!

"When we got there, the lady that she was beating on said, 'That's all right. That's all right. This woman is a nurse, and she has had Guillain-Barré syndrome for four years. All these years, her arms have hung down uselessly at her side. She has been unable to raise them.'

"While she was lying on the floor laughing, the power of God hit her, and she was totally healed. She was laughing so loud and so hard that she couldn't say anything, so the only way she could show the friend who brought her was to beat on her, so the woman could see that she had got strength back in her arms!

"Then, we went back on the stage and discovered that all twenty of them on the floor were laughing! All of them were just absolutely having hysterics. They started out just like I did that night at the Full Gospel. Pretty soon, some people in the audience began to laugh; then, everybody in the audience was laughing! So I looked at Charles and I said, 'If you can't beat them, join them!' We didn't have holy laughter; we were just laughing at them because they looked so funny out there.

"Finally, the laughing stopped, and the woman who had been taking care of the book table for us ran up and said, 'Last year, I had a mastectomy. While we were laughing tonight, God grew a whole new breast on me.' Hallelujah!

"We went home that night not understanding anything that went on. The next morning, I called Dr. Lester Sumrall, who is a very good friend of ours and has been for years. I said, 'Dr. Sumrall, you've got to tell me what happened last night.' I told him about all those crazy things that were going on.

"He said, 'Frances, what you experienced in your service was holy laughter. Anything that is of God is holy, and anything that is holy has power; and it also has healing power along with it.'

"Anything that is of God is holy, and anything that is holy has power; and it also has healing power along with it."

"You know, sometimes we don't encourage something because we are afraid of it. We were a little afraid, because there is always somebody who has to get in the flesh. So we didn't squash it, but we most certainly did not encourage it, although we experienced little outbreaks over the years.

"Then, I never heard another thing about holy laughter until December of last year. Pastor Karl Strader of the great Carpenter's Home Church in Lakeland, Florida, called us up and said, 'Frances, you've got to come down here! I have Rodney Howard-Browne, and in his services, everybody laughs and laughs and laughs!'

"I asked, 'For what?' It didn't make sense to me. I thought, *What are they all laughing about?*

"He said, 'Rodney has been here for thirteen weeks this year, and I tell you, the people are just laughing! I spent six weeks lying on the floor myself doing nothing but laughing!'

"'Really?' I asked. I have to be honest with you. It didn't make sense to me at all, but here goes that hunger again! You know, whenever it is of God, there is that little desire in there.

"Charles and I decided that we were going to go down, and we were going to take a look at this man who made everybody laugh. Maybe he was the world's greatest comedian, I don't know, but we were going to go down and we were going to see exactly what this was. They had the peanut fares on, so we took our secretary and her husband along with us for a penny apiece so that they would see it, too.

"We sat there in the next-to-last service on Thursday night. We went Thursday night and Friday night, the last two meetings. Would you believe nobody laughed? How many of you think God has a sense of humor? See, God knows when He wants to show you something.

"Nobody laughed! I looked over at Pastor Strader, who told me that he had spent six weeks on the floor laughing, and he is sitting there with the most solemn look on his face. He didn't laugh one time. I didn't laugh. Charles didn't laugh. Barbara didn't laugh, and her husband didn't laugh. Well, that was a disappointment!

"But I saw power that I have never seen before! I saw a young man who ministered in signs, wonders, and miracles that were absolutely incredible!

"We went back the next night. Would you believe nobody laughed the second night? Not one person laughed the second night! Now, here we had spent all this money to go down and see holy laughter, and nobody laughed.

"At the end of the second night, he asked for all the pastors and all of the evangelists to come forward because, he said, 'I want to impart this gift to you. I want each of you to take it wherever you go.'

"Now, Charles and I went up because he had asked for evangelists to come forward. He laid hands on us, and we both went under the power. I felt absolutely nothing. I didn't laugh. Charles didn't laugh. Neither did any minister laugh that night, did they, Charles? Everybody was lying on the floor, and nobody was laughing. But as he laid hands on Charles and me, he said, 'New beginnings. New beginnings.'

"I am not moved by what I see, hear, feel, taste, or smell. I am moved by what the Word of God says, and I am moved by what a man of God says. He said, 'New beginnings, and I impart to you this gift of holy laughter.'

"Some of you may have been at Carpenter's Home Church. You can always tell when an architect is a man; he never builds with consideration for a woman. Falling down under the power in that church slants downhill to the first pew, and then it goes up. So when they lay hands on you and you fall, you are lying on the floor with your feet above your head!

"This might be all right for you young people, but I just had my seventy-eighth birthday last Sunday, hallelujah! It is not too easy to get off of the floor when you are that old—especially when you are at an angle like that. I thought, *I hope somebody sends a forklift or something to get me up!*"

Frances paused for a moment to catch her breath and spotted Pastor Lee and his wife splitting their sides with laughter!

"If anything would have made me laugh," she continued, "that would have—trying to figure out how I was going to get off of the floor. But, praise the Lord, they sent about ten men, and they managed to get me up off the floor. Now as I said, I didn't feel the wind of the Spirit. I didn't feel the power of God go through me when Rodney Howard-Browne laid hands on me. I didn't feel anything, but I received what he said.

"I just receive everything that God has for me. When something unusual begins to happen, don't criticize God."

"You see, I just receive everything that God has for me. So Charles and I went home, and unusual things began to happen. Now, when something unusual begins to happen, don't criticize God. Don't say, 'Don't dump it in my box. It can't happen that way.' Let God do what He wants to do.

"I was sitting in my office, just like I sit every day when I am at home, and the receptionist came running in. I was on the telephone, and she came running in, and she said, 'Frances, take this call.' She didn't wait until I got off of the phone. She said, 'You have to take this telephone call! This man is going to commit suicide! I think you had better handle it.'

"I said, 'Okay,' because I always take the ones that are critical. I got on the telephone, and this man had tic douloureux. That is what is called the 'suicide disease' because it is the most severe type of pain known to man. This man was telling me what agony he was in, how he couldn't stand the stabbing pains, and how he was going to kill himself; and I yelled, 'Don't you do it! Don't you do it!'

"I began to pray. I have more fun in church than anybody I know. When I got saved, I read in my Bible that Jesus said, 'I have come that your cup of joy might be full.' (See John 15:11.) And my cup of joy has been running over ever since then.

"But when I pray, especially in a life-and-death situation, there is no one in the world who is any more serious than I am. I said, 'Satan, I bind you right now by the Spirit of God, in Jesus' name. You foul stinking spirit of suicide, I command you to come out of him, in the name of Jesus.' I started to come against the spirit of tic douloureux, and this man went, 'Haw, haw, haw!'

"He started laughing on the telephone. It was so loud that it actually scared me. I took the telephone away from my ear, and my secretary ran into my office and asked, 'What's the matter?'

"I said, 'This man is laughing on the telephone!'

"Charles heard him from out in the hall, and he comes running in to see what was the matter with me.

"I said, 'I prayed for this man. I am commanding the spirit of suicide to come out, and he is laughing!'

"I am not used to having people laugh at me when I pray. Here we are—I'm holding my telephone at arm's length, he called our 1-800 number, I am paying for the call, and he is laughing and laughing. I let this go on for five minutes while I said, 'Thank You, Jesus! Thank You, Jesus! Thank You, Jesus!' because he couldn't hear anything that I had said. Finally, after five minutes, I decided that had been long enough, so I hung up the telephone!

"The next day, he called back and asked for me personally. He said, 'I want you to know that I have not had a pain since you prayed for me yesterday!'

"I was so excited! This was wonderful! Now, I want you to know that since then, he has been back to the hospital. He has had all the CAT scans, the MRIs made, and there is no scar tissue on his brain; there is not a sign of tic douloureux left in his body! Hallelujah!

"The next day, I got another telephone call, and this one was from a lady from London who had flown over to the United States. She was coming to Houston to ask me to pray for her, and she said, 'I am at the JFK Airport on Long Island, and I am in such pain that there is no way I can get to Houston. Please pray for me now, because I am going to go to the hospital.'

"She was dying of cancer, so I commanded that spirit of cancer to come out! I commanded that spirit of death to come out! And I did all the things that we do for cancer. I cursed the seed and I cursed the root, and all of a sudden, this woman began to laugh and have hysterics on the telephone.

"Maybe you are smarter than I am, but I did not connect the two things together. I was praying so fervently on the telephone, and this woman was just laughing and laughing and laughing. Finally, she said, 'I don't have any pain!'

"With that, we hung up. Then, I got a call, I guess it was three days later, and she had checked into the hospital, and they had found no trace of cancer! I thought, *Isn't that wonderful? God just heals them on the telephone, and this woman didn't even have to come to Houston!*

"Well, on the third day, I got another telephone call. It was from a very good friend of ours, and she said, 'I just want you to know that I sent you one thousand dollars for a memorial fund for my cousin's daughter. She is dying, and they pulled the plug on her, so it will be just a matter of hours until she is gone. I am going over to be with my cousin, and I wanted to call and let you know so that I could tell them I had given a memorial gift.'

"I said, 'Look, why don't we pray for a living memorial instead of a dead one?' How many of you think that is much better? This girl had been in a coma for seven weeks. I bound the devil and commanded that girl to come out of her coma, in the name of Jesus. I spoke the other things. I spoke the scar tissue off of her brain in the name of Jesus—and remember that every miracle that occurred was in the name of Jesus because of the power that is in the name of Jesus—and right in the middle of all this, how many of you know what she began to do? She laughed and laughed and laughed!

"Every miracle that occurred was in the name of Jesus because of the power that is in the name of Jesus."

"We finally hung up, and I still did not understand the laughter behind each of these calls. At first, I thought those people were hysterical because they were in pain and hurt so badly, and so forth.

"The next day, she called me back and said, 'Do you know what? Within one hour after you prayed for her to come out of that coma, the doctor was in her room, and she sat up on the side of the bed and said that she was hungry and wanted something to eat.'

"The doctor said, 'She is still in a coma; she's out of her mind. She can't eat anything.'

"The lady said, 'I am not! I am hungry, and I want something to eat!'

"Two days later, she went home. She was taken from intensive care to a regular room for one day, and they kept her there for one day before sending her home. She is back at work, and there is not one single, solitary thing wrong with her. Hallelujah!

"Finally, I said, 'God, if You want everybody who calls this office to laugh, that's all right with me. When I pray for them and I'm so serious and I command that spirit of death to come out, if You want that to be their response, that's all right with me.'

"Now here is the interesting thing: I have never had another call where the person laughed. I had four that one week, and I've forgotten what the fourth one was, but it was another life-and-death situation where the person laughed and then was totally healed. I said, 'God, You really are doing a new thing, aren't You?'

"You know, we need to be responsive to the things of God. I asked God and I said, 'You know, God, I have all these Scriptures on joy, and

I have them on happiness, but would You give me one Scripture on holy laughter? One is all I need; just give me one that I can stand on, in Your Word.'

"So I picked up my Bible, and, once again, God put something new in there that I had never seen before. It was in the book of Psalms, which I have read over and over and over again because I love the book of Psalms. It was in Psalm 126:

> *When the* LORD *brought back the captivity of Zion, we were like those who dream. Then our mouth was filled with laughter, and our tongue with singing.* (verses 1–2)

"I said, 'God, this must be a version I have never read!' No, it was the same one I had read all the time.

> *Then our mouth was filled with laughter, and our tongue with singing. Then they said among the nations, "The* LORD *has done great things for them." The* LORD *has done great things for us, and we are glad.* (verses 2–3)

"I said, 'God, You are the one that fills our mouths with laughter!'

"We went to England and were there over the Easter holidays. If you know the English people, you know that they are very formal, and they are very reserved. The pastors over there are very staid and stiff, and their church services are very formal. But God said to me, 'You share this message.'

"All the way through the service, the audience was listening to everything I said. Right at the end, the spirit of holy laughter just fell on a lady. She was way back in the corner. And the holy laughter sounded beautiful.

"I turned around to the pastor. Oh, thank God for boldness! I laid hands on this beautifully immaculate, well-groomed young man, very dignified, very reserved, and about forty years of age. I said, 'What you need is a good dose of Holy Ghost laughter!'

"I've never seen anybody do what he did. I mean, he looked at me for a split second and then went, 'Haw, haw, haw!' This was the very dignified English pastor! And then he fell onto the floor and laughed for two solid hours. We have videos of all of this, of this pastor lying on the floor, pounding on the floor, and beating on the floor. He tried to get up five times!

"The next day, he said to his congregation, 'When God puts you there with holy laughter, stay there and enjoy it! I did my best to get up five times, and I couldn't get up. I would have been smart to just lie there and enjoy every minute of it.'

"He rolled, and I mean *rolled*, on the floor! There he was, this very formal Englishman, but we imparted to him a fresh anointing. He went down to Brazil the week after we were there, and I hear that he turned Brazil upside down! They said the power that they saw, the healings that they saw, the signs and the wonders that they saw, were beyond and above anything they had ever seen in the nation of Brazil. And he said, in his ministry, that he had never seen anything to compare with the anointing that had been placed on him.

"We spoke two weeks ago in Denver. There were thirty-seven foreign nations represented there. All the people from the foreign nations came up, and they said, 'Lay hands on us! We want to take it back.' So holy laughter is in Ireland, Scotland, Switzerland, and Holland. It is in Nigeria, Uganda, and South Africa. I mean, it is all over the place!

"The other night, we had a blind man in our service, and he laughed himself into sight! Absolutely laughed and laughed and laughed, and suddenly his sight returned. We also had a deaf man, and he laughed and laughed and laughed, and suddenly he jumped off the floor and put his hands on his ears and said, 'I can hear! Everything is so loud!' You know, when you come from total deafness and all of a sudden you can hear, everything sounds like thunder in your ears!

"I think it is the neatest thing I have ever seen. People get supernaturally healed while they are laughing."

"God is doing something fantastic. I don't understand it at all. I absolutely and completely do not understand it, but I think it is the neatest thing I have ever seen. I think it is wonderful, but what we are also seeing is an increase in healing. People get supernaturally healed while they are laughing."[7]

[7] Frances Hunter, *Holy Laughter* CD (Kingwood, TX: Hunter Ministries). Used with permission.

Chapter Twelve

Take a Census of the World

Five years of Healing Explosions throughout the world is much easier on a thirty-five-year-old evangelist than on one who is about to turn seventy. Several years before the Explosions started, Frances became so exhausted that she thought God was going retire her from overseas travel. Then, God healed her of diabetes and she got a new rush of energy that propelled her through over a hundred national and international Healing Explosions. Charles was always by her side, making sure that her strength was reserved for ministry alone, but by 1990, Charles and Frances both realized that it was time to cut back on the pace of the Healing Explosions.

On March 31, 1990, the Lord spoke to Charles in the midst of a service at a small church in Austin, Texas. He did not have an opportunity to share with Frances until late that afternoon that God had told him, "Take a census of the world." They did not question the Lord but trusted Him for divine guidance.

Three weeks after Frances' seventieth birthday, on Tuesday, May 29, 1990, she was sitting at her desk in Houston when the Lord said to her, "Go back to Honduras on Thursday and set things in motion for the first census ever held in the world where a nation will have the gospel preached to every creature in the country." When she told Charles, he said, "Let's go!"

The Honduras Census

Frances scheduled plane tickets and made a hurried phone call to a young man named Luis Sorto, who had worked with them in Honduras.

She shared the word that God had given to Charles and God's directive for Honduras to be the first nation in the world to have the gospel preached to every single individual in a matter of a few days. She told him that they would be there on Thursday to begin discussing the logistics of the census.

The Hunters' Healing Explosion in Honduras had made their name well-known across the tiny nation. Before the Explosion, thousands of copies of the book *How to Heal the Sick*, plus hundreds of video healing schools, had been sent to train healing teams there. The huge stadium had been filled with more than forty-five thousand people, including over six thousand who had been trained to serve on healing teams. The signs and wonders that occurred had been reported by Christian and secular media alike and had left an indelible imprint on the nation. Their contacts could hardly wait for them to return.

When Charles and Frances landed in Honduras, they were met by eager pastors who had already made arrangements for a large pastors' meeting on Saturday. Over two hundred and fifty pastors from Pentecostal and non-Pentecostal denominations, including Catholic, agreed to lay down all differences and work together in the effort to reach the entire nation in a two-week period.

A meeting was planned to teach people how to be effective witnesses for Christ. The Hunters purchased ten thousand copies of *The Four Spiritual Laws* booklet in Spanish for the pastors to use. Representatives from the Billy Graham Evangelistic Association and Bill Bright's Campus Crusade for Christ agreed to participate in the training effort.

Evangelistic Census advertisement in Honduras.

The population of Honduras at that time was five million. The goal for the census was to win two million or more people to Jesus in a two-week time period and begin weekly Bible studies through home cell groups to mature them in their Christian walks. The census would take place between January 5 and January 19, 1991, culminating with a harvest celebration on January 19.

Charles studied how the United States government performed the national census every ten years. He learned that each state was divided into sections. Then each county, city, and town was divided into zip code areas and then into neighborhoods within the zip code. Census workers were able to methodically visit every neighborhood and every home in the nation.

These principles were put into place in Honduras. They divided the eighteen states into districts, and each district was then divided into smaller units that could be systematically reached by evangelistic census workers. East district had a director who recruited individuals to contact all the pastors in their assigned areas. The directors were trained to lead people to Jesus. They watched the *How to Heal the Sick* videos. They were even taught how to dress properly when calling on the pastors.

An audiotape sharing the vision was prepared for every pastor who participated. Half a million Spanish *Living New Testaments* were purchased. Forms were printed for recording the names of every person who received Jesus.

Workers were trained to go out two by two, following the example in Luke 10:1 when Jesus sent out His disciples. Each team was taught how to lead individuals to Jesus and pray for their needs. They learned how to fill out the forms that would provide an accurate count of how many had been contacted and how many of those had received Christ.

Each team was to go to its assigned area of about thirty-five houses and knock on every door. If no one answered, the team members would make a note of it and return later until they had contacted every person in their district within the two-week census period.

Whenever the gospel was presented and someone was saved, that person would be invited to join a home cell group. The team leaders were trained to act as leaders of the cell groups under the umbrella of the local church, if there was one. Audiotapes or videotapes with basic Christian living principles in harmony with all denominations would be

Whenever the gospel was presented and someone was saved, that person would be invited to join a home cell group.

used at the cell groups. All salvation forms were to be turned in each day and would be passed along to the directors and on to the census headquarters.

An Explosion of Souls!

Seven months of pastors' meetings, organization, training, and ordering and printing materials passed quickly, and on the appointed day in January 1991, the evangelistic census workers were launched all over Honduras. Each team knew exactly which thirty-five homes they would contact each day of the two-week census. They knocked on doors and asked several nonthreatening questions as they had been trained to do. At the appropriate time, they asked if the individual would like to ask Jesus into his or her heart, and if the answer was affirmative, they had the individual repeat a short prayer of salvation. They asked if the resident was a part of a local church and then invited him or her to a cell group for Bible study.

On January 19, when the forms had all been counted, over two million people in the nation of five million had asked Jesus Christ into their hearts. The impact of what had been done through the efforts of ordinary laypeople was phenomenal. Not only were souls saved, but churches also exploded. Reports began coming to the Hunters of new ground breaking ceremonies and new buildings being needed all over Honduras.

Before the census, Pastor Roberto Ventura of Gezarim Church had three hundred members in his congregation. Several years after the census, his church was ministering to four thousand people. Their organization had fifty churches before the census and eighty-six afterward. Vida Abundante Church exploded from seven hundred members to six thousand in just a few years. The Foursquare Church in San Pedro Sula had two hundred members before the census and, by 1998, was reaching the lives of fifteen thousand people.

When God gave the Hunters an impossible task and they unquestioningly said, "Let's go," He supplied the organizers, the pastoral cooperation, and thousands of laborers to go two by two and take a nation for Jesus. Charles would often explain, whenever someone asked how God could use two old people like them to do such incredible things, "When God tells us to do something, we're just dumb enough to obey Him."

Charles would often explain, "When God tells us to do something, we're just dumb enough to obey Him."

Win Your City to Jesus

When the Honduras census was over, the Hunters excitedly communicated with pastors of large churches all over the United States and shared the outstanding results of the Honduras outreach. In 1992, they mobilized a national campaign to "Win Your City to Jesus."

Many pastors who were passionate about winning souls caught the vision, and mega-churches trained teams to go door-to-door in designated zip code areas of their cities. Thousands of believers learned to witness to complete strangers. There is no way to measure the extent of this campaign's effect on the lives of believers for generations to come in giving them the confidence to share their faith.

After months' worth of expenses from coast-to-coast travel, printing, duplication, and mailing, the Hunters' office was stacked with bills, bills, and more bills. By the end of the year, they were nearly two hundred thousand dollars in debt.

The ministry had nowhere near the amount of funds needed to pay all the bills, so Charles and Frances emptied their personal savings account and even withdrew their retirement funds to pay off the debt. They believed that they had no choice but to do the right thing and owe no creditors.

When Charles came into Frances' office holding a check for the last of their life savings, Frances took the fifty-five-thousand-dollar check and tossed it into the air, as if into God's hands, and watched it drift down to the floor. She proclaimed, "God, I trust You with my soul, so I certainly can trust You with my finances!" Charles picked up the check and deposited it into the ministry account.

On the way home, they stopped for two bowls of soup and some corn bread, using the last of the cash in Charles' wallet. Once home, they were completely exhausted from their emotionally trying day and went directly to bed. As they snuggled up to each other, they agreed, "This really makes you trust God, doesn't it?"

It was not the most joyous time in their lives, yet they both felt closer to God and to each other than they ever had before. Before going to sleep, Frances did say to Charles, "Please don't die, honey, because we don't have enough money to bury you!" The next instant, both of them began to laugh as though that was the funniest thing they had ever heard! They knew God would come through, and He did.

In the Air Again

The doors of the former Soviet Union had opened. Charles and Frances did not know how long there would be an opportunity to go into Russia with the gospel, so they moved quickly. If they had any thoughts of slowing down, they swept them from their minds! They made several trips to Russia, forming alliances with strong pastors who could help them train additional pastors and start churches, which were desperately needed to satisfy the hunger of the people who had been spiritually starved for seventy years.

The Hunters provided television sets, VCRs, and videotapes in the native language. They encouraged churches in the United States to sponsor new churches in Russia. They analyzed the costs and calculated that twenty-five hundred dollars could provide a television and videotape player with fifty-two hours of Bible teaching in Russian. Video Bible Fellowships popped up all over Russia.

By 1994, Video Bible Fellowships expanded into Asia. The Hunters had a year's worth of videotapes translated into Mandarin and Cantonese for speakers of these two major Chinese dialects. They were also translated into five major languages for the people of India. Charles and Frances traveled throughout the United States raising money for the tens of thousands of dollars expended each month to spread the gospel and birth new churches for masses of people overseas.

In 1996, they hired a World Evangelistic Census Director, Ron Kite, who assumed the burden of overseas travel for them. He flew to Russia and various nations in Africa, Asia, and South America, sharing the vision and making new contacts. For the first year, the reports of salvations merely trickled in. But then, God gave the Hunters a fantastic tool to win people to Jesus.

There Are Two Kinds of...

Frances was seated in a restaurant with a group from the small Missouri church where she and Charles were about to minister. A gentleman came over to the table and sat down next to her. She did not know who he was, and when she later inquired of the others at the table, no one else had seen him, even though he had been seated in an obvious spot next to Frances.

The gentleman exchanged a few comments with her, and then he said, "Frances, I know how much you've always loved winning people to Jesus, and I want to tell you about a new way and demonstrate it to you."

Charles and Frances were always anxious to learn about new ways to lead people to Jesus because that was the burning desire of their hearts, so Frances gave him her full attention.

He went on, "As soon as the waitress gets to the table, she will ask what we would like to drink, and I will say, 'Water.' Then I will say, 'Now, may I ask you a question? Did you know that there are two kinds of waitresses—those who are saved and those who are about to be? Which one are you?'"

> *"Did you know that there are two kinds of waitresses—those who are saved and those who are about to be?"*

Something exploded inside of Frances because the question didn't give the person a way out of answering. She instantly saw it was a "win/win" situation! The person would either answer "I'm saved" or "I am about to be."

Frances eagerly responded, "Don't you do it! Let me try it on the waitress!"

When the waitress came over to the table, she asked what Frances would like to drink. Frances answered, "I'd like water, please. Now, may I ask you a question?"

The girl answered, "Yes."

Frances reached for her hand and gave her a warm smile as she asked,

"Did you know that there are two kinds of beautiful waitresses who work in this restaurant—those who are saved and those who are about to be? Which one are you?"

To Frances' amazement, the waitress started crying and said, "I guess I'm the last one."

Frances responded, "Wonderful! Repeat this after me: Father, forgive my sins."

The waitress said, "Father, forgive my sins."

Frances said, "Jesus, come into my heart and make me the kind of person You want me to be."

The waitress repeated, "Jesus, come into my heart and make me the kind of person You want me to be."

Frances continued, "Thank You for saving me today."

The waitress said, "Thank You for saving me today," and burst into tears.

Frances asked, "Where is Jesus right now?"

The waitress answered, "In my heart!" She was so moved by what she had experienced that she left, crying, and it was several minutes before she returned to wait on them again. She had someone with her and said to Frances, "Give him what you gave me!"

Charles and Frances had never experienced a soulwinning method this quick and easy. They led people to the Lord in parking lots, restaurants, hotel lobbies, elevators, and airports. Whenever they went to the grocery store, no matter how small the item was that they purchased, they always asked the employee who bagged their groceries to carry their packages to the car. Charles would ask, "Did you know that there are two kinds of executive bag boys who work at this store?" and would lead him in asking Jesus into his heart before they reached the car.

I'm a Muslim

One evening, the Hunters went to a hotel restaurant to have a late dinner after a meeting. They had to go through the bar area to get to the dining room.

Charles noticed a waitress coming out of the bar and told her, "There are two kinds of people who work in a dining room and who also have to work in a bar—those who are saved and those who are about to be. Which one are you?"

She answered, "I am a Muslim."

Charles said, "There are two kinds of Muslims—those who want to go to heaven and those who want to go to hell."

She said, "I want to go to heaven."

Charles had her repeat the prayer and then asked her, "Where is Jesus?"

She answered, "In my heart!"[8]

No Wrong Numbers

A friend of the Hunters had a rewarding telephone experience using the "two kinds of" method. Her phone rang, and when she answered it, the person did not recognize her voice and apologized, saying, "I'm sorry, I must have dialed the wrong number."

She replied, "No, you got the right number even if you dialed the wrong number. There are two kinds of people who dial wrong numbers—those who are saved and those who are about to be. Which one are you?"

The man answered, "I guess I'm about to be, because nobody has ever asked me that question before." He repeated the prayer, asking Jesus to come into his heart, and before they hung up, he thanked her repeatedly for asking him the "two kinds of" question. He said, "Until today, no one has ever asked me if I knew Jesus."

Yes, It Works

As the Hunters ministered on the "two kinds of" method across the country, pastors who had never led anyone to the Lord experienced the joy of seeing people saved. People in the congregation were challenged to win someone to the Lord and bring that person to church that night. People who never thought they could witness effectively began leading complete strangers to invite Jesus Christ into their hearts.

---

[8] Charles and Frances Hunter, *There Are Two Kinds Of...* (Kingwood, TX: Hunter Books, 1997), 24.

Some doubters wondered if such a tool could really work. "Was there really a salvation experience? Could the person's life really be changed?" they asked.

The power is in the name of Jesus, and to invite Him into the heart is to say yes to the drawing power of the Holy Spirit, wherever and however it may happen.

The Hunters found that it worked just as powerfully as if the person had sat through a three-hour crusade or revival service and then went forward to invite Jesus into his or her heart. The power is in the name of Jesus, and to invite Him into the heart is to say yes to the drawing power of the Holy Spirit, wherever and however it may happen. Charles and Frances always instructed the people to read their Bibles and get involved in a good Bible-based church, just as an altar worker would have done after a soulwinning event.

Does It Last?

One morning, Frances and Charles were at a food stand in the Tampa airport, they ordered a plate of nachos for breakfast. Frances asked the young server, "Do you know there are two kinds of beautiful young waitresses—those who are saved and those who are about to be?"

The waitress answered, "I suppose I'm about to be."

Frances took her hand and said, "Repeat after me: Father, forgive my sins." The girl repeated the words.

"Jesus, I invite you to come into my heart." She repeated the statement.

"Thank You, Jesus, that I am saved." When the girl repeated this last line, a big smile broke through the drawn expression on her face, and her eyes sparkled. It was obvious that she had felt something wonderful happen inside her spirit.

They came back to the same nacho bar the following year, and the same young lady waited on them again. They were looking at their tickets to make sure they knew exactly what time their plane would take off when Charles noticed that a waitress had come over to them. He immediately asked, "Did you know there are two kinds of wonderful waitresses in this restaurant?"

The girl laughed and said, "You got me last year, remember? And would you like to know what happened?" She proceeded to tell them how asking Jesus into her heart that day had helped her to refocus her entire life. She excitedly shared all that God had helped her to sort through and work out during the past year.

The Hunters returned to the Tampa airport nacho stand about a year later. This time, the young lady ran up to them and hugged them as if they were her mother and father. She said, "You may not remember me, but I know you, and God has done such awesome things in my life that all I can do is praise Him—all because you led me to Jesus three years ago!"

The Hunters eventually authored a booklet entitled *There Are Two Kinds Of...*, and churches across the nation ordered copies. One can only imagine how many people used this simple evangelizing tool to expand God's kingdom.

A Breakthrough in the World Evangelistic Census

When the Hunters shared the "two kinds of" message with the World Evangelistic Census Director, he immediately began to incorporate it into every conversation he had with pastors, leaders, and contact persons in the nations where he was working. He sent scores of WEC packets around the globe, each one including the *There Are Two Kinds Of...* booklet. He flew to Kenya, Uganda, Zambia, South Africa, Zimbabwe, Mauritius, Brazil, Colombia, Uruguay, Argentina, Russia, Ukraine, the Philippines, New Zealand, India, and China.

When the hosting pastor picked him up at the airport, Ron demonstrated the "two kinds of" message with every person they had contact with on the way to the hotel. Cab drivers repeated the prayer and got saved. Baggage clerks got saved. Hotel doormen got saved. Hotel housekeeping staff members got saved. If the hosting pastor had any doubts before he picked up the WEC director, he didn't have any by the time he got to the hotel. Sometimes, four or five people would ask Jesus into their hearts between the airport and the hotel.

One day, Ron was sitting with one of the India census directors and a number of pastors at a table in a restaurant in India. The enthusiastic Indian director asked him to show the others how to lead someone to Jesus, so when the waiter came over to the table, Ron said, "There are two kinds of waiters in this restaurant—those who are saved and those who are about to be. Which one are you?"

The waiter answered, "I am Hindu."

Ron responded, "There are two kinds of Hindus…" and had him repeat the prayer to ask Jesus into his heart. After the waiter repeated the prayer asking Jesus into his heart, he stood there with absolutely no emotion or indication that he had understood anything. After he left, all the pastors were completely silent, and Ron thought, *Oh, no. This is what I came to teach them, and I blew it.*

They paid the bill without a word, exited the restaurant, and walked toward the car. Before they had gotten very far, the Hindu waiter burst through the door and ran across the parking lot to catch up with them. With his face beaming, he shouted, "I got it, I got it! Jesus is in my heart!"

The pastors could not deny what they had witnessed. There was no explanation except for the power in the name of Jesus and that when someone asks Jesus into his or her heart, the life of the Holy Spirit bears witness that something wonderful has changed on the inside.

National Directors Multiply the Vision

Once a pastor had seen how simple it would be to train his people to win the lost, the next step was for the people in the church to get trained and have a "practice" census before the international director left for the next country.

The directors in each nation were chosen because of prior involvement with the Hunters, because of long-term credibility as pastors of major ministries, or because of divine connections that occurred one after another. As each person saw for himself how powerful the "two kinds of" witnessing tool was, he would start training people within his own church and then begin to network, meeting and communicating with other pastors and training them and their congregations so that the vision multiplied.

As each person saw for himself how powerful the "two kinds of" witnessing tool was, he would start training people within his own church and then begin to network, meeting and communicating with other pastors so that the vision multiplied.

The director for each country would set up a census office with the understanding that the work would be supported by his own nation. The Hunters sent a monthly offering to the major directors to help with printing expenses and postage and to purchase duplicating equipment and videotapes for video home churches. However, the nationals were responsible for networking, training, doing door-to-door outreaches, and collecting completed salvation forms. They would report monthly to Hunter Ministries, and ongoing records were kept for all areas of the world.

It's Easy to Win a Million Souls!

The first substantial census figures came from the Philippines, where the Filipino national director had a network of more than a thousand pastors. He continually moved about through the islands. Many of the regions were so remote that they could be reached only by motorcycle; others could be accessed only by boat or on horseback. He seemed possessed with the vision, and he communicated to the home office that "it is easy to win a million souls!" He had favorable contacts with certain radio stations, which would play the Hunters' taped messages at no charge.

The WEC director made several trips to the Philippines and was always amazed at the eagerness of the people to do the census. They would fill buses to their maximum capacities, drive to the designated areas, and knock on the doors of houses or, in many cases, small huts. But it was the vast networking among pastors that brought about the successful results.

The census that had seemed to do nothing in 1997 took off like a rocket all over the world once the "two kinds of" method was introduced. Reports came in that were staggering: tens of thousands, hundreds of thousands, and then millions of salvations were counted. The national directors had been trained and were required to collect forms for each census to document the number of people who had accepted salvation.

By the turn of the century, when the reports came in for tens of millions, and then hundreds of millions, the numbers seemed unbelievable. The Lord gave Frances a Scripture that seemed to explain what was happening:

> *Look among the nations and watch; be utterly astounded! For I will work a work in your days which you would not believe, though it were told you.* (Habakkuk 1:5)

What About the Numbers?

The numbers of saved people continued to grow, and the work was going on in more nations than could be visited or personally overseen by the WEC office. Thus, there was a natural concern about the accuracy of the documented salvations. With so many people involved, there was a margin of error to consider, as well as other potential human flaws in methods of data collection and reporting. But it was decided that it was better to trust God and believe in the reports that were e-mailed or faxed daily from nearly one hundred nations than to limit God with unbelief.

Although Hunter Ministries no longer maintains an office dedicated to the World Evangelistic Census, they still receive reports from all the nations that were involved, along with updates on salvations and video home churches. At the time of this writing, 1,000,626,754 souls had been reported as having been saved because of the mandate God gave to Charles in 1990.

In the Philippines, crowds followed them wherever they went.

Perhaps only the bookkeeping angels of heaven know whether the number is totally accurate, but it is undisputed that, through the World Evangelistic Census, a hundred nations were ignited with a growing passion to win the lost, several thousand home video churches were started, and existing churches doubled, tripled, and quadrupled in size—all because a wild soulwinner and a spiritually turned-on CPA said, "Let's go!"

For the Value of One Soul

It was 1983, and Charles and Frances had just arrived in Tokyo, Japan. Their eyes widened in appreciation of the "land of the rising sun" as their host drove past colorful pagodas and maneuvered the car through busy streets to their hotel. They could hardly wait to meet the little group of Christians who had invited them. They checked into their hotel and hurriedly unpacked a few things to prepare for their impending miracle service.

At the service, the Hunters were introduced to a pastor from Taiwan who gave them an enthusiastic welcome. He was also a very prosperous businessman who owned a restaurant at the entrance to the busiest subway in the world. He had sponsored the meetings and would sponsor them in Taiwan, as well. Even though he did not speak English, they had an instant rapport. When he invited Charles and Frances to lunch, they had no interpreter with them, so they all spoke in tongues. The joy of the Lord radiated around the table and, although no one could understand a single word, their spirits communicated fluently.

A year later, a tired-looking Asian pastor arrived at a service in New Jersey where Charles and Frances were ministering. He was soaking wet and stood shivering at the entrance to the small auditorium. As soon as he caught his breath, he moved toward the stage.

In Taiwan, the pastor had been diagnosed with cancer and had been advised to get all of his affairs in order because he had only a short time left to live. He did not accept the bad report and responded, "No, I will go to the United States. Charles and Frances Hunter will pray for me, and I will be healed." He had flown to Los Angeles and, through an interpreter, learned from the Hunters' office where they were ministering.

The Los Angeles Airport had directed him to LaGuardia instead of Newark, so after landing in New Jersey, he had to take a train, a bus, and a taxicab to get to the church. However, the church where they had been scheduled to speak had not been able to open yet because of a delay in obtaining a permit. The meeting had been relocated to another building a block away. The cab departed after dropping off the Taiwanese pastor at the church, and he had to walk the long block in the pouring rain.

When he saw Charles and Frances ministering, he hurried to the stage and handed Charles a note describing his problem. They could see that he had lost a lot of weight and looked terribly sick. They immediately prayed for him and commanded the root and seed of every cancer cell to die in the name of Jesus and for all pain to go, in Jesus' name.

The pastor fell to the floor. Frances said he looked like a corpse as he lay motionless under the power of God. After this meeting, the Hunters had five more meetings in New Jersey, and he came up at every service to have them lay hands on him. Then, he went back home. Several weeks later, the Hunters received a letter from Taiwan. The letter contained a statement from the pastor's doctor saying that he no longer had any sign of cancer. The doctor must have been a Christian, because he acknowledged that his patient had received a miracle from God.

Several years went by. Charles and Frances were getting ready to minister at Melodyland Christian Center in California when a woman came over to them and told Frances that someone was there with a gift for her but wanted to give it to her in private. The sanctuary was not yet open to the public, but the woman opened the door for them to walk inside. There stood their Taiwanese friend in glowing health. Beside him was his daughter, a beautiful girl who spoke perfect English and had just graduated from Vassar College.

She held out a little package to Frances and said, "My mother died, and my father had given her this ring for her sixty-fifth birthday. When she died, my father called the children in and told them that he was going to give Mother's ring to Frances Hunter." Children of the Far East are extremely respectful of their parents' wishes, and they accepted their father's decision graciously.

When the daughter handed the ring to Frances, she looked at it and almost fainted because she had never seen a diamond that big. Frances said, "No, this belongs to you, because it was your mother's." She tried to hand it back to the girl.

The young woman smiled warmly and said, "No. It is for you."

Frances accepted the exquisite ring and, as soon as possible, had it adjusted to fit her ring finger perfectly. She and Charles renewed their marriage vows as Charles placed the ring on Frances' finger. It instantly became one of Frances' most treasured possessions—not just because of its size or its beauty, but also because of the special memories and the love that accompanied it.

One day in November 2003, Charles and Frances stopped at the store on their way home from the office to pick up a few groceries. It had been a tiring day, and Frances walked over to a bench where she could sit and wait while Charles paid for the groceries. She straightened her dress as she sat down and suddenly panicked to see that her ring from the Taiwanese pastor was not on her finger. As soon as Charles came over, she told him her ring had fallen off somewhere. Charles called for the manager and asked if he would ask some employees to search the floor throughout the store for Frances' ring because it was very precious to her. The ring was not found.

Charles and Frances went back to the car. They checked under the seats and searched the interior of the vehicle but found no ring. Then, they drove back to the office. They looked over, under, in, and behind everything in the office. The ring was not found. They looked in the parking lot. No ring. At home, they searched the floors and the furniture and went through every article of clothing Frances had worn recently. They examined every nook and cranny where they imagined the ring might have fallen or rolled. The ring was not found.

After several weeks, Charles said, "Honey, let met buy you another ring. I can't buy you one as big as the other one, but I love you and I want to get you another one."

Frances said, "No; God is going to give me that ring back. I'm asking God every day to have an angel put the ring where I will see it."

Six months passed, and one day, when they were not as busy as usual, Frances felt that the office needed a little housecleaning. Her secretary began to help her sort through old files, and they began to throw out those that were between ten and twelve years old. They pitched some files into the trash without examining them but searched others to see if they contained anything important.

The only explanation was that God had answered her prayer and had had an angel place the ring right in front of her.

Suddenly, Frances opened one folder and saw, right in the middle of the folder—which had not been taken out of the filing cabinet for at least ten years—her diamond ring! There was no explanation except that God had answered her prayer and had had an angel place it right in front of her. Frances screamed, "I found my ring! I found my ring!"

Charles shouted, "Thank You, Jesus!"

Frances called Joan. She called Tom. She called family members and friends all over the country so that everyone could rejoice with her. The treasured ring that had been lost was now found! Jesus told a similar story to His disciples to illustrate the value of one soul:

> *A woman has ten valuable silver coins and loses one. Won't she light a lamp and look in every corner of the house and sweep every nook and cranny until she finds it? And then won't she call in her friends and neighbors to rejoice with her? In the same way there is joy in the presence of the angels of God when one sinner repents.*
>
> (Luke 15:8–10 TLB)

The life that the Hunters have lived has been lived for the value of one soul. Every waking moment has been geared toward winning that one whom the Lord would lead to them each day. God was able to use them to win millions because they were faithful to win one.

Chapter Thirteen

The Astrodome Retires in Glory

Charles and Frances were both excited beyond words to be planning their final, large-scale Healing Explosion at the Reliant Astrodome in Houston. In 1965, the giant arena had opened with a Billy Graham crusade. When Ron called to reserve a date for the Healing Explosion, he learned that the famous coliseum was available for just one more weekend before it would be retired. It would hold a few minor concerts and high school football games in the future, but the Healing Explosion would be the last notable event to be held in the building.

Interestingly, the Astrodome would be the Hunters' 172nd Healing Explosion, and at the time of the event, they would be a combined age of 172 years. The date was set for October 2, 2004.

The Hunters began promoting the Astrodome Explosion with their monthly Opportunity Letter. They rented advertising space in *Charisma*, a widely circulated Christian magazine. Their office sent out promotional packages to churches across the nation. They received enthusiastic endorsements from T. L. Osborn, Marilyn Hickey, R. W. Schambach, Benny Hinn, Mark Chironna, Rodney Howard-Browne, Richard Roberts, Norvel Hayes, Robb Thompson, Doug Stringer, A. L. and Joyce Gill, Dodie Osteen, Kirbyjon Caldwell, and others. Many of these people arranged their schedules so that they could join Charles and Frances on the platform on October 2.

Coordination for the Explosion was a massive endeavor. The staff of the Hunters' home office, Ron Kite in the Oklahoma office, and the

Hunters' daughter, Joan, all worked together to ensure this historic event would take place like clockwork. Joan met with pastors all over the southwest and appeared on the Daystar Television Network with her parents or took their place whenever they were unable to appear for interviews in person. She had been in ministry all of her adult life and, once her four daughters were grown, had begun her own healing ministry. She could hardly contain her excitement because this explosion would include a transfer of her mother's anointing over to her so that she could take God's healing power to the nations of the world.

On October 2, 2004, the Reliant Astrodome became a living heartbeat with the energy of God. Thousands of cars jammed the streets leading to the stadium. Crowds of expectant men, women, and children wove their ways into the giant, domed arena. Many had been to one or more of the Hunters' previous Healing Explosions; others came looking forward to experiencing God's power for the first time. The atmosphere was charged with anticipation. As people filed in to take their seats, Joe and Becky Cruse led praise and worship, lifting the faith and expectancy to even higher levels.

Charles and Frances entered the arena through the doors at the rear of the platform. They made their way to the stage and slipped into comfortable armchairs for the service. As they surveyed the incoming crowd of people, they held hands in joyous expectancy. They had not conducted a major Healing Explosion in the United States for ten years. Tonight, they would again have the opportunity to encourage the body of Christ that God's power was intended to work through ordinary believers when they were obedient to do what Jesus had commissioned them to do.

God's power is intended to work through ordinary believers when they are obedient to do what Jesus commissioned them to do.

Frances then stepped up, took the microphone, and expressed her belief that the Astrodome Healing Explosion would be a catalyst for healing to gain a greater emphasis in the church across the nation and throughout the world.

One after another, guests who were seated on the large stage came to share how the Hunters had impacted their own ministries. Long-time friend Betty Tapscott had been at the Hunters' Bible study when the Lord first spoke to Frances about the Astrodome. A. L. and Joyce Gill shared how the Hunters had made them totally dissatisfied with their comfortable places in the business world and motivated them to take God's power into more than seventy nations. Marilyn Hickey, Dodie Osteen, Norvel Hayes, Mike Francen, and a host of renowned ministers all took turns at the microphone, as did representatives from several nations, including Canada, England, Zimbabwe, and Brazil.

When Geneto Alencar had first heard of the Astrodome Explosion, he had said, "There is nothing in this world that can keep me away from this service." Fifteen years before, Charles and Frances had gone with him from one end of Brazil to the other, sometimes ministering until midnight and leaving for the airport at four o'clock the next morning. Frances had prayed for his wife to have a child, and young Gineto II stood beside his father on the stage.

Full Gospel Businessmen's Fellowship president Richard Shakarian concluded the impressive assembly of guests as he spoke of the powerful impact Charles and Frances had made in the charismatic renewal and his fond memories of the Hunters' relationship with his dad, Demos, who had founded the FGBMFI.

Houston Mayor Bill White was unable to attend, but he sent a proclamation naming October 2, 2004, "Charles and Frances Hunter Day" in Houston. The proclamation from the mayor's office brought tears of joy to Charles and Frances' eyes and cheers of appreciation from the audience.

The Baptism with the Holy Spirit

Frances had the microphone again. It was time to give people the opportunity to be filled with the Holy Spirit. She had to breathe rapidly to keep pace with the excitement in her heart. Occasionally stopping to catch her breath, she prefaced the upcoming baptism service by sharing how Charles had begun to have back problems in February 2003 and how he had endured month after month of unsuccessful surgeries. She praised God for His faithfulness during that exhausting year and related that, finally, most of the pain had subsided and that Charles had regained enough strength to walk up onto that platform with her. She looked over at Charles and smiled at him as if she were a new bride beaming at her bridegroom.

With the sound of triumph in her voice, Frances continued, "Now, I would like for every single person in this building who wants Jesus to baptize you with the Holy Spirit to get up and run down front. Come on, right now! Hallelujah! And Charles will lead you in receiving the Holy Spirit!"

As had happened at every other Healing Explosion, it was astounding to see the huge proportion of the audience that rose from their seats and quickly made their ways down to the edge of the platform. More than half of the giant arena's floor was packed with people, crowding as close to the stage as they could get.

The arena became silent with expectancy as Charles Hunter rose from his armchair and walked to the microphone. Those who had seen him minister the baptism of the Holy Spirit dozens, if not hundreds, of times were overjoyed to see him once again do what he was known for all over the world.

Charles held the microphone and smiled encouragingly at the people before him. His feet were steady and the anointing of God was upon him as he began to speak:

"You are about to receive what the Bible calls the baptism with the Holy Spirit, or the gift of the Holy Spirit. Your spirit, the same size as your body, is about to be filled completely with God's Spirit, and just like Jesus instructed, you will speak in a spirit language as the Holy Spirit gives the utterance.

"All languages are made up of a bunch of different little syllable sounds. We must make the sounds, but the Holy Spirit will give the utterance or the language. It's a miracle! It's a sign and wonder that Jesus said would follow every believer.

"We are going to ask Jesus to baptize us with the Holy Spirit just as sincerely as we asked Him to save us. He will do His part, but we must do our part. Paul said that he prayed with his 'thinker' or understanding, but he also prayed with his spirit.

Jesus will baptize us with the Holy Spirit. He will do His part, but we must do our part.

"When you pray with your spirit, you do not think of the sounds of the language. Just trust God, but make the sounds when I tell you to. In just a moment, when I say, 'Now,' begin loving and praising God by speaking forth a lot of different syllable sounds, but not in English.

"At first, make the sounds rapidly so you won't try to think as you do in speaking your natural language. Continue making the sounds with long, flowing sentences. Don't just make a few sounds and stop and start. Let them flow like rivers of living water!

"Repeat this after me," Charles said, and he led the group one statement at a time:

"Lord Jesus, thank You for the most exciting gift on earth—the gift of salvation. Jesus, You promised another gift—the gift of the Holy Spirit. So I ask You, Lord Jesus, to baptize me with the Holy Spirit, right now, exactly like on the day of Pentecost. Thank You, Jesus. You have done Your part. Now, I am going to do my part. I am going to lift up my hands to God. And when Charles says 'Now,' I am going to begin to praise God, but not in any language I know, because I can't speak two languages at one time. Father, I love You. I praise You. I worship You. I love You with all of my heart.

"Ready? One. Two. Three. Now!"[9]

Charles began to pray in tongues, and a multitude of people across the arena floor spontaneously prayed in tongues along with him. He showed them how to pray loudly and how to pray softly. He directed them to stop. He guided them to start again. He showed them that they could sing in their new language. Thousands in the stands joined the chorus and praised God enthusiastically and adoringly. As suddenly as the crowd had begun speaking in tongues, they stopped. The arena basked in the presence of the Holy Spirit as Charles returned to his seat and the people on the floor returned to theirs.

Healings and Miracles

After everyone was seated, Frances spoke about the Great Commission Jesus gave to believers in Mark 16:15–18. She relayed the passion that had guided her and Charles for more than thirty-four years—the passion to train ordinary believers that they are commissioned to do the works that Jesus did, and even greater works, too, because of the power of the Holy Spirit within them. She reminded the thousands before her that it was not Charles and Frances' power but the power in the name of Jesus that

[9] Charles Hunter, *How to Receive and Minister the Baptism with the Holy Spirit* (Kingwood, TX: Hunter Books, 1989), excerpts pp. 7–13.

brought healing and miracles, and "if Charles and Frances can do it, you can do it, too!"

Then, she prophesied, saying, "This Healing Explosion is going to start a healing revival all over the United States of America. We believe as a result of the Healing Explosion that every church in America is going to have a healing school. It's time we got over dead church services! It's time to get into a realm where the Spirit of God moves in every service, where people are healed in every service, where you see God changing lives wherever you go."

Frances then gave the cue for all of the healing teams to come forward. From every aisle, more than a thousand healing teams descended the steps and streamed down to the arena floor. There were many more than the 120 that she had envisioned three decades ago in that little home Bible study. As they spread out so that others could get to them easily for ministry, the entire floor of the arena was dotted with enthusiastic believers who had been trained to be extensions of the hands of Jesus.

At the beginning of the evening, Greg Smelter, a retired football player for the former Houston Oilers, had testified that he had been healed as he walked into the stadium. He said that the anointing of God was so strong that there was no need for anyone to lay hands on him. Now, scores of others filed to the stage to give their testimonies of how God had touched them through the hands of the healing teams.

People lifted once-stiff arms or moved knees, legs, or hips without pain. Some bent over to touch the floor or twisted and turned in happy demonstrations of their healings.

A child who came to the service deaf could now hear normally. A little boy who had been losing his eyesight was able to see clearly. People lifted once-stiff arms or moved knees, legs, or hips without pain. Some bent over to touch the floor or twisted and turned in happy demonstrations of their healings. Frances and Charles knew from all their prior experiences that many healings would not be visible that night and that there would be a flow of phone calls and letters to their office with many more testimonies once people had returned to their doctors for verification of the miraculous results.

The buzz of voices gradually came to a close; the Hunters were escorted to the bus that was waiting for them outside. The lights were dimmed in the Reliant Astrodome. It was a glorious way for a grand stadium to end its thirty-nine years of service to the city of Houston.

All of Charles and Frances' family attended the Healing Explosion at the Astrodome in 2004.

Chapter Fourteen

Until Jesus Comes

The Astrodome may have retired, but Charles and Frances Hunter had no such intention. The fact that they were no longer flying all over the nation did not mean their passion for spreading the name of Jesus, praying for the sick, and training believers to do the work of the ministry had lessened. They began conducting monthly healing seminars in the church that housed their offices. Their meetings were—and are to this day—held on the second weekend of each month, with one service on Friday night and two services on Saturday. Often, guest ministers come to join the Hunters in teaching and laying hands on the sick.

The fact that they were no longer flying all over the nation did not mean their passion for spreading the name of Jesus had lessened.

When God Doesn't Do It Your Way

When the Hunters first started their healing ministry, Frances would sometimes be asked, "If God heals, why do you wear glasses?"

Her consistent answer was, "So I can see!" She then used the question as an opportunity to teach, saying, "If you have a bridge, you don't need to walk on water."

Whenever Frances encountered a life-threatening disease or injury, God healed her. She had files of doctors' reports with X-rays and blood tests to verify the miracle-working power of God in her body. But, He allowed her to wear contacts and glasses to receive perfect vision. He allowed her to use a walker for her foot.

The Hunters encountered life's challenges just like everyone else to whom they ministered. They used their faith to receive many miracles, and no matter what happened, they always continued with their travels, their Healing Explosions, their books, and all that God put into their hearts. They praised and thanked God for the miracle they were expecting and testified through their joy and perseverance, "God is faithful!"

A New Approach to Ministry

Early in 2003, Charles and Frances had a combined age of 168 and were still enthusiastically involved in full-time ministry. Although they no longer traveled overseas, they made occasional trips within the continental United States, conducted local healing seminars, and were frequent guests on Christian television programs.

They sold the ministry's property and relocated to the office of a new Spirit-filled church near their former location. The pastor was Larry Ansel, and his wife, Sheila, had been dramatically healed of Lupus when Charles and Frances first met the couple and prayed for Sheila in a grocery store parking lot. The Ansels were thrilled to welcome the downsized Hunter Ministry offices to their church building.

It was a blessing for the Hunters to be free from the responsibility of maintaining their former building and property. They reduced their office staff to the basics. Beth Carley, who had proved her loyalty and commitment to the Hunters for many years, continued her office duties and learned to take on additional responsibilities. Others were hired from time to time as needed. Charles and Frances answered prayer requests with letters, phone calls, or e-mails. Frances never tired of writing books. Their Web site was continually updated and their office continued to ship materials around the world for DVD home churches and healing schools. Every day was one of anticipation and joy.

In Sickness and In Health

In January 2004, Frances went to the doctor for a routine physical checkup and a mammogram. She received an alarming report that she had a large lump in her left breast, and her doctor ordered a biopsy procedure immediately. When the report was returned, the surgeon's office called Frances to come in and discuss the results.

The morning Frances was supposed to go for her appointment, Dr. Goldfedder, a retired neurologist who was now healing people by laying hands on them, called her. He shared that he had a strong feeling from the Lord that when she saw the doctor, she should not ask him, "How are you?" but should instead ask, "How are you feeling today?"

Frances entered the doctor's office and had waited only a few minutes when he appeared at the door. She cheerfully asked him, "How are you feeling today?"

A bit surprised by her question, the doctor hesitated a second, then responded, "Well, my neck is killing me. I was scheduled to have surgery, but I put it off so I could take care of you."

"Neck problems are easy for God!" Frances exclaimed. Then she suggested, "Since you are so tall, would you mind kneeling so I can reach your neck?" He came over and knelt on the floor, and she placed her hands gently on his neck, her fingers touching right along his spinal column, her thumbs in front of his ears.

She said, "In the name of Jesus, I take authority over all these vertebrae and discs. I command you, in Jesus' name, to go into position and be healed. I command all muscles, nerves, ligaments, and tendons to be strengthened and healed and, in Jesus' name, I rebuke all pain!"

When she finished, the doctor stood up, moved his head and neck in every direction without pain, and asked in amazement, "Will it always feel this good?"

"Hallelujah!" Frances said with a laugh.

The surgeon moved toward the counter to pick up Frances' biopsy report. Before he could give it to her, she asked him, "Have you ever asked Jesus into your heart?"

"No, I haven't," he responded.

"Would you like to right now?"

He said, "Yes, I would."

"Repeat this after me," she said. "Father, forgive my sins. Jesus, come into my heart and make me the kind of person You want me to be. Thank You, Lord, for saving me." The surgeon repeated each sentence after Frances. Then she asked him, "Where is Jesus right now?"

"In my heart," he answered. His eyes met hers with a thoughtful gaze, and he continued, "You don't know how much I needed this. My mother and father died last month."

He cleared his throat, sat down across from Frances, and opened the report in his hand. "Frances, the biopsy is positive. That means it is malignant. I want you to go right to the hospital. I have already made the arrangements for you."

Frances was so excited about the surgeon praying to ask Jesus into his heart and getting healed that she had forgotten to pray for herself.

Frances was always looking for opportunities to lead someone to Jesus.

As soon as she was settled in her hospital room, Frances began looking for opportunities to lead someone to Jesus. Whenever she or Charles had been in a hospital for any reason, they always had revival. The nurses got saved, the orderlies got saved, and they would bring other people around to get Charles or Frances to pray for them. Someone shared with her that the surgeon she had just led to Jesus was Jewish. Frances could only rejoice at God's divine timing for his life.

When the time for the surgery arrived, she was wheeled into the operating room. As the cool liquid anesthetic flowed into her veins, Frances drifted to sleep, still thanking God for the doctor's salvation.

When she awoke, she sat up in bed, and if there had not been physical evidence of the mastectomy, no one would have believed she had just undergone surgery. She received a good report—the cancer had not spread—and she miraculously experienced no pain, either then or throughout her recovery. The nurses kept offering her pain medication, but Frances repeatedly insisted, "I don't need it! I don't need it!" She also refused radiation and chemotherapy, and, in the five years that have passed since her surgery, she has never experienced any recurrence of cancer.

A day after the surgery, Frances picked up the phone and called Ron

Kite. As though nothing had happened and she were sitting at her desk at the office, she exclaimed, "God just spoke one word to me: Astrodome! Get it for our next Healing Explosion!"

People who had known Frances, regardless of how long, often commented that she was the only person they knew who could direct the ministry and dictate a new book from a hospital room or plan a Healing Explosion the day after a radical surgery. Frances truly seemed unstoppable, and two things never wavered under any circumstances: her zeal for the Lord and her devotion to Charles.

The Ordination Services

In April 2006, Charles and Frances received a mandate from God to hold an ordination service. As leaders of an incorporated ministry, they had ordained many ministers over the years, but they had never ordained a large number of people at one time. In deciding to have an ordination service, they agreed that to hold an event of this nature was a sacred trust that they did not take lightly. Their ultimate goal was in line with their lifelong vision—to spread the gospel and equip believers to continue the ministry.

Both Charles and Frances had followed strict guidelines of integrity throughout their lives and expected all the candidates for ordination to have high standards of honor and commitment. They prayerfully considered each applicant and made personal calls if they had questions, doubts, or a need for clarification.

When this process was complete, two hundred applicants had been approved for ordination. The ordination service was preceded by hours of training—one session on Thursday, three sessions on Friday, and three sessions on Saturday. Of utmost importance to the Hunters was the responsibility of those who were to be ordained. Frances charged the group, "There is no 'halfway' with God. You are either totally committed or not."

"There is no 'halfway' with God. You are either totally committed or not."

Most of the people who came to be ordained were already involved in teaching, healing, or music ministries. Some were on staff in their churches or worked with various ministries as volunteers. Charles and Frances believed that ordination would give them the confidence to reach out into their realms of influence in even greater ways, some perhaps to accept full-time ministry callings.

The first ordination service brought forth an eruption of positive responses. Charles and Frances could see that their vision of multiplication was working, and a second ordination service was scheduled for October 2007.

The National Day of Healing

At the beginning of 2006, the Holy Spirit gave Frances such a sensational idea that she was amazed she had not thought of it before: a National Day of Healing. It would be a day when churches of every denomination would open their doors from eleven o'clock in the morning until two o'clock in the afternoon to allow people from the community to come and have trained healing teams lay hands on them. The date was set for October 28, 2006.

The Hunter Ministry Web site invited churches and laypeople alike to participate in the National Day of Healing. If a nearby church did not participate, believers were encouraged to view the *How to Heal the Sick* training materials themselves and use their home or other available venue to minister to people on October 28. Among the first to announce that he would be a part of the momentous outreach effort was Cal Pierce, director of 432 John G. Lake Healing Rooms across the country. Daystar Television Network fully endorsed the National Day of Healing, followed by a host of other ministries that did the same.

In order to encourage small churches to get involved, Hunter Ministries sent a Healing Packet free of charge to every church of two hundred or fewer members that requested the package. The packet included a seven-hour *Power Pack* (the condensed version of their fourteen-hour *How to Heal the Sick* video), a *How to Heal the Sick* book, a training manual called *Handbook for Healing*, and a CD entitled *Healing Is for You.*

Several long-time friends helped to spread the word about the National Day of Healing. Steve Strang, publisher of *Charisma* magazine, ran an article that went to tens of thousands of homes and ministries. Frances taped several radio programs with Sid Roth and flew to Charlotte, North Carolina, to tape a television program with him. Pastors in many nations e-mailed the Hunters asking if they could participate. Frances' response was, "Yes, yes, yes!"

Daystar Television volunteered their studio to host the Houston portion of the event on October 28. Lakewood Church volunteered to help in any way they could, sending ushers, language coordinators, parking attendants, and prayer teams. God even volunteered, providing not only His miracle-working presence, but also a gorgeous Houston day on which the hurricane predictions for the area were not fulfilled.

An Avalanche of Good Reports

Daystar only had two phone lines in their station, so Lakewood Church set aside twenty-five phone lines to take incoming testimonies then e-mail them to Daystar. For the first two and a half hours on the Day of Healing, not a single report came in to the Daystar studio. Frances and Charles began to wonder if anything was happening at all, either in the U.S. or anywhere else in the world. Late in the third hour, a problem with e-mail was discovered, and once it was fixed, the station was flooded with testimonies.

Curry Juneau's church in Houston reported that a man who had been confined to a wheelchair for years but who had started walking early in the service and kept on walking, non-stop, for two hours. In New Jersey, a kidney-sized tumor on someone's wrist totally disappeared. In Ft. Wayne, Indiana, more than a thousand people showed up for healing, and those newly freed from their pains began running around the building as no one had ever done in that church.

People newly freed from their pains began running around the building as no one had ever done in that church.

In Columbus, Ohio, a man named Mick had been ill for twenty years without a specific diagnosis. His family had sought help from neurologists and doctors in many fields. At fifty years of age, he was confined to a wheelchair and was unable to care for himself or communicate. On the National Day of Healing, his mother checked him out of the nursing home where he lived and drove him to the local church. She had trouble finding the location, but they finally arrived, and she prayed they weren't too late.

The healing teams first took authority over demonic spirits. They walked Mick through receiving Jesus as his Savior, and then he was baptized in the Holy Spirit. Several teams ministered persistently with Mick until he got up from his wheelchair and took two steps, unassisted. His entire countenance brightened as he realized what he had done, and he walked effortlessly toward his mother. As onlookers began to weep in the presence of God, he took off and ran so fast that the pastor could hardly keep up with him!

Seven Cornfields Down the Road

A helicopter pilot who had been in an accident had undergone several surgeries, followed by four years of chiropractic treatments. The chiropractor finally told him that he could do nothing else for him but recommended that he attend the healing service being held in a little church located "way out in the sticks."

"They're having some kind of National Day of Healing out there," he said. "Why don't you go out and see what happens? You haven't got anything to lose." The man called the church and got directions similar to this:

> You go down State Road 22 until you come to a barn that has been burned down. Go about fifty feet farther, and you will see a little country road that goes off to the right. Turn right, go down three cornfields, and after you pass the third cornfield, turn left. Go approximately half a mile, and you will run into a big maple tree. Turn right at the maple tree, and go seven cornfields down. When you go past the seventh cornfield, turn back right again for about half a mile. Then, you will see two little ruts going down a road. Turn left on this road and go to the end of the road. When you come to the end of the road, you will see a little church there, and that is where the healing service is being held.[10]

Since the helicopter pilot was driving and not flying, it took him three

[10] Charles and Frances Hunter, *What's New?* (Kingwood, TX: Hunter Ministries, 2006), 9–10.

hours to find the church. When he went inside, there were six people, two of whom were lying on the floor. He had seen people fall on a Benny Hinn program before and thought, *That's really fake if I ever saw anything.* But the next thing he knew, he was lying on the floor! He lay there for several minutes as if pinned to the floor before he could get up. When he finally was able to stand on his feet, he discovered to his amazement that the pain that had made him miserable for many years was totally gone. Before he left the tiny group, he was also saved and filled with the Holy Spirit!

The National Day of Healing was historic. It was nothing short of a Healing Explosion multiplied. E-mails and faxes continued to pour in to Lakewood Church and Hunter Ministries for weeks following the event. People wrote that they were healed of varicose veins, emphysema, fibromyalgia, and carpal tunnel syndrome. Churches reported Down syndrome healed, blind eyes receiving sight, and people previously confined to wheelchairs leaving them.

The National Day of Healing was historic. It was nothing short of a Healing Explosion multiplied.

Exciting testimonies came in from Pakistan, South Africa, the Philippines, Brazil, India, and many other nations that had humbly asked if they could be involved in what they thought was a "U.S. National Day of Healing." The Hunters decided that their next National Day of Healing would be held on September 22, 2007—and that it would be called a "Worldwide Day of Healing!"

I Will Live to Declare the Works of the Lord

When the year 2000 arrived, a lot of people who were perfectly sane wondered if something earthshaking was going to happen, either natural or supernatural. Some, who might be considered a little flaky, went to the mountaintops to camp out and await the return of Jesus. Seconds, minutes, and hours ticked by without the blessed sighting of the Lord. As the weeks passed without these individuals' being raptured, they meandered back to their humdrum lives and tried to recalculate when the Lord will finally take us all away to heaven's rewards.

Charles and Frances Hunter are so in love with Jesus that they would jump for joy if He came at any moment. But their love also tells them that every minute He leaves them on this earth is to be well spent, just as Charles and his brother's dime was well spent when they went to the carnival and bought a bunch of bananas. Each day that passes without Jesus' return means one more day to win a lost soul, a day to send a *How to Heal the Sick* packet to a tiny church in Montana, a mega-church in Denver, or a village in Kenya, or a day to hold a healing seminar or an ordination service.

Each day that passes without Jesus' return means one more day to win a lost soul.

The year 2007 was an exciting one for the Hunters. In April, a third ordination service launched new ministers and birthed new works around the world. On September 22, God's power traversed nations through the Worldwide Day of Healing. The Hunters quickly announced the date for the next Worldwide Day of Healing: September 20, 2008.

Before the end of 2008, God gave Frances a gift of immeasurable value. For more than thirty-three years, she had longed to see her oldest grandson, Brant, one more time. This was Tom's son, and Tom and his wife had separated when the child was just two years old. After the divorce, Frances had lost contact with them.

On August thirteenth, Frances' daughter Joan received a phone call from a friend with Brant's contact information. She was in shock as her friend spoke the words, "I found your nephew. I've already talked to him. Would you like his phone number?" Before Joan could make the call, her phone rang again, it was Brant's mother, Jan. Brant had called her because he had found out that his aunt was trying to find him.

God brought Frances a desire of her heart—her grandson. Soon after their first contact, Brant flew to Houston for a visit. For the first time since Brant was two years old, he spent Christmas with his grandmother and other long-lost family members.

May 8, 2008, was Frances' ninety-second birthday. She beamed with excitement as her staff coaxed her into the church auditorium, where she was greeted by long-time friends from many parts of the country. She delighted in the scores of pink balloons, pink flowers, pink presents, and pink streamers. July 23, 2008, was Charles' eighty-eighth birthday. They are both fulfilling Frances' confession—they are alive, praising God, and declaring the works of the Lord.

Conclusion

By the start of 2007, Charles and Frances had attained the collective age of 176, and their doctor strongly suggested that they stop traveling. Catching an early flight on Friday morning, ministering in four or five services, and then returning home on Sunday had to come to an end.

Not being able to travel restricted the Hunters' ability to minister in local churches all around the world as they had done for thirty-seven years, yet Charles and Frances were not disheartened. They knew that God had a plan. Not traveling gave Frances more time to write inspiring and stimulating new books and make bigger plans for the Worldwide Day of Healing in the fall. Frances was one of the few people over ninety years of age who continued to make plans for the unforeseeable future.

Setting in squeaky wooden rocking chairs on the front porch and rocking their days away until Jesus comes was not God's intent for Charles and Frances. When they no longer traveled to the people, the people came to them. God had mandated that Charles and Frances ordain people and send them forth to fulfill the Great Commission. God brought people to Texas from all over the world to an older couple who understood what it meant to be totally sold out to Jesus. The ministry has continued in its extraordinarily teaching and has kept reaching out to people in great numbers.

As of August 2008, Frances is ninety-two years old and is behind her desk, finishing up details for the September 20, 2008 Worldwide Day of Healing. Twenty states currently have healing schools in the United States, along with foreign schools in East Africa, South Africa, West Africa, Australia, Canada, and the United Kingdom.

The work of the Lord continues into the twenty-first century. Charles and Frances Hunter are examples of God taking unlikely candidates and making them world changers. In many ways, the Hunters are like the Apostle John. He was the only apostle who did not die a martyr's death. He lived into his nineties and encouraged people until the very end of his life. God continued to use him because of his strong faith. Many scholars believe that John was in his later years when he wrote the books that bear his name and the book of Revelation. He was strong until the end. He finished well. Charles and Frances Hunter are finishing well.

About the Authors

Richard Young is a former educator, businessman, and pastor. The son of a Free Will Baptist pastor, Richard started preaching at fourteen and pastoring at twenty. He comes from a great heritage of preachers and pastors, as there has been a member of his family in the ministry consistently since 1876. Richard has been a writer all of his adult life, writing corporate training manuals and collegiate self-study courses, as well as two textbooks. He has written articles for both Christian and secular magazines and journals. His previously published biographies are *The Rise of Lakewood Church and Joel Osteen* and *The Journey of T. D. Jakes.*

Richard received Bachelor of Arts and Master of Science degrees from Southern Nazarene University in Bethany, Oklahoma. He has completed the coursework for his doctorate in education at Oklahoma State University. He served as vice president of academics at American Christian College and Seminary in Oklahoma City as well as dean of academics at Oklahoma Junior College. He also was a trainer for Century 21 across the state of Oklahoma.

Coauthor Brenda Young holds a Bachelor of Science degree in Speech and Communications and a Master of Performing Arts from Oklahoma City University. She has written and produced many Christian children's plays, founded a children's theatre with a large cast, and been a professor of speech, humanities, and drama. During the time she and Richard were in the pastorate, she developed a Fine Arts preschool for children in a low-income area, giving the children a safe place to be creative. Later, she became the director of the church food pantry, where two thousand families per month receive groceries.

Brenda and Richard have been married for more than three decades. Although they find great joy in helping people, their highest delight is spending time with their three children and nine grandchildren.

The Rise of Lakewood Church and Joel Osteen
Richard Young

He was the most unlikely of protégés—a young man with no college or seminary degree and virtually no preaching experience. Yet, Joel Osteen was handed the reins of his father's lifelong ministry when John Osteen died suddenly in 1999. Witness the miraculous rise of Lakewood Church from humble beginnings in a Texas feed store to becoming the largest church in America. From the life and times of Joel Osteen, you will learn the power of vision, humility, integrity, and facing adversity with faith. Never again will you doubt what God can do with those who are fully devoted to Him!

ISBN: 978-0-88368-975-2 • Hardcover • 272 pages

Handbook for Healing (revised edition)
Charles and Frances Hunter

In this recently updated and expanded edition, Charles and Frances Hunter present the keys to healing that they have found in the Bible and through the innovations of medical science. Written as a complement to the their best-selling *How to Heal the Sick*, this book is essential for your library—and your ministry. Discover that God can use you to bring healing and help to family, friends, and everyone you come in contact with. No longer will you have to stand by, helpless, when people are hurting!

ISBN: 978-0-88368-705-5 • Hardcover • 224 pages

How to Heal the Sick
Charles and Frances Hunter

A loved one is sick...your friend was just in an accident...a family member is facing an emotional crisis. Have you ever desperately longed to reach out your hand and bring healing to these needs? At times, our hearts ache with the desire to help, but either we don't know how or we are afraid and stop short. The truth is that, if you are a Christian, the Holy Spirit within you is ready to heal the sick! Charles and Frances Hunter present solid, biblically based methods of healing that can bring not only physical health, but also spiritual wholeness and the abundant life to you, your family, and everyone around you.

ISBN: 978-0-88368-600-3 • Trade • 224 pages

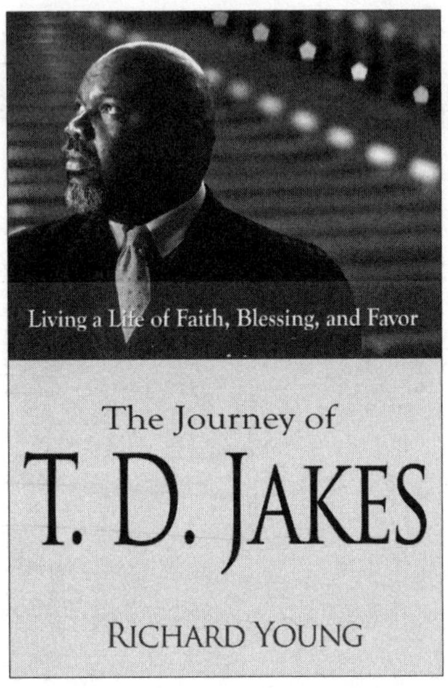

The Journey of T. D. Jakes
Richard Young

Discover the lessons Thomas Dexter Jakes learned as a young boy growing up in Appalachian poverty. Experience the victory and redemption of a young man who faced—and overcame—the seduction of drugs and crime. Witness his rise from pastor of a tiny rural congregation to the leader of a 30,000-member megachurch in one of America's largest cities. You, too, can live a life of faith, blessing, and favor. Most important, you will witness the biblical truth: "*With God all things are possible*" (Matthew 19:26).

ISBN: 978-1-60374-069-2 • Trade • 224 pages